Shoperapy

By: Stephanie Scott

Copyright © 2025 by Stephanie Scott

All rights reserved. No part of this publication may be reproduced, stored, or transmitted in any form or by any means, electronic, mechanical, photocopying, recording, scanning, or otherwise, without written permission from the publisher. It is illegal to copy this book, post it to a website, or distribute it by any other means without permission.

This novel is entirely a work of fiction. The names, characters, and incidents portrayed in it are the work of the author's imagination. Any resemblance to actual persons, living or dead, events, or localities is entirely coincidental.

Stephanie Scott asserts the moral right to be identified as the author of this work.

Stephanie Scott has no responsibility for the persistence or accuracy of URLs for external or third-party Internet Websites referred to in this publication and does not guarantee that any content on such Websites is, or will remain, accurate or appropriate.

Designations used by companies to distinguish their products are often claimed as trademarks. All brand names and product names used in this book and on its cover are trade names, service marks, trademarks, and registered trademarks of their respective owners. The publishers and the book are not associated with any product or vendor mentioned in this book. None of the companies referenced within the book have endorsed the book.

First edition Editing by Sarah Linke
This book was professionally typeset on Reedsy.

Find out more at reedsy.com

Acknowledgements

As I sit here, writing the final page of my first novel, I find myself overwhelmed by a mix of emotions. This book has not merely been a dream come true; it has been a fabulous journey filled with laughter, and an undeniable connection to the incredible people who have been a huge part of my life.

To my family: Tony, Rebecca, Daniel, Hannah, and Adam, I owe a debt of gratitude that is impossible to put into words. Your amazing love and support provided me with the encouragement that allowed me to pursue my dream. The daily conversations and check-ins, gave me the push I needed. Thank you for believing in me and giving me the space to write. I love you all.

To my mum, who never once doubted that I could write this book, thank you for believing in me! To my grandfather, the first writer in my family, for giving me the writing gene. I hope I have made you proud!

Then, there are my amazing friends. How do I possibly thank you? Your presence in my life has provided me with countless experiences worth writing about, from stories of friendship over the years to the countless mishaps and all things fabulous. You know who you are, my amazing friends; you have given me the adventures to inspire every chapter of this book.

To my editor, Sarah, thank you for being my guiding light and believing in me and encouraging me to write not one, but four books! Your constructive feedback transformed my manuscript from a rough draft into a polished piece of art. Your insights were not just critiques; they were gifts that opened my eyes to new perspectives and possibilities.

A massive thank you to Sophie, my publisher at British Book Publishers. You took my ideas far beyond what I had envisioned for this book. Your enthusiasm and belief in my work brought my manuscript to life in a way I hardly dared to dream. You've turned my manuscript into a polished work of art that I'm proud to share with the world.

I cannot overlook the little things that have made all the difference during the writing process. To Nescafé, your endless supply of caffeine was crucial to this book's completion. Those mugs of hot coffee, also accompanied by a dash of energy in the form of chocolate biscuits, often pushed me through those late nights and early mornings when the words just wouldn't flow. How grateful I am for the comforting ritual of a cup of coffee when immersed in my writing.

Lastly, to the amazing females whose lives intersected with mine, thank you for the laughter, love, and everything in between. Your stories, your mishaps, your heartbreaks, and your friendships fuelled the pages of this book, creating stories from experiences that most women can relate to. You have filled my life with humour and love. Thank you so much for being my muse.

As I close this chapter of acknowledgements on my first book, I am reminded that this book is only the beginning of an even larger adventure to share with all of you. I hope the pages to follow can reflect the friendship, love, and laughter you have all showered upon me and inspire others in their own journeys, to dream big!

Love Stephanie xxx

About the Author

 Stephanie Scott lives in Scotland and is married with four gorgeous children. She is a Depute Head Teacher and has worked in Education for almost 30 years. Her passion has always been writing since she could hold a pen. It has always been her dream to write a fun novel that women could relate to.

She loves all things fabulous: family, friendships, fashion and fun.

You can connect with me on:

http://instagram.com/stephaniescott_author

Prologue

Posted: 4:43 AM (GMT)

User: Your Fashion Ellie-vator

Subscribers: 0

Out with the Old, In with the New: Aka Goodbye Men, Hello Strong Female Friendships! (and Killer Heels!), or The Start of a Love that Won't Leave Me Crying on the Curb: Shoperapy, a Fashion Boutique with Purpose

Good morning, you! Yes, you, Gorgeous! Gor-ge-OUS! It's a little early, I know. Even my coffee machine was like, "Ellie, it's 3 am. Coffee machines need their beauty sleep, too, don't you know?" But I'll tell you what I told my coffee machine: I'm sorry! I'm just so free-kin excited. And no, this second cappuccino has nothing to do with it.

Today, in fact, in a mere six hours, I will be cutting the ribbon on my very own fashion boutique. You know what? Scratch that. Our very own fashion boutique. You know what? Scratch that, too! Your very own fashion boutique.

Because with some gorgeous heels and some sturdy advice and encouragement, I want Shoperapy to be the place to help you find love. All of you out there. Every single one of you. Dreams come true for all you inspiring, incredible, wow-oh-wow women.

Me?

I'm over it. Done with it. Could not be less interested in it. I've forsaken it. Yes, love. Fore-sworn it forever and ever. And ever. (And ever!)

Oh, believe me. It's not for lack of trying, ladies. I've had two 'Meet the Parents' kind-of-serious relationships, the requisite drunken one-night stand (or two or three – that I can remember), the flings, the 'Let's Move In, No Never Mind, the Let's Break Up's, the rain kisses, the rain fights, the rain roll in the hays, the cheaters, the liars, the good for nothings, the, in a word, men.

I don't know, maybe a black cat walked across my love sign. Or my soulmate walked under a ladder and a piano fell on his adorable (I'm sure) head. Or it was just gusty the night our twin flames were born. Who knows, really?

But that doesn't mean you shouldn't find love! You deserve love. Each and every one of you. And it is out there somewhere, waiting for you, ladies. And I'm here to help you find it (or at least look and feel like a million dollars when you do.) Not only will I find you the perfect outfit, but the perfect outfit for the perfect one, or the perfect one, for now.

Pinky promise.

Well, I'd love to stay and chat some more, but I should probably go now. Lots to do before the Grand Opening! And I could really use another cappuccino right now. It's only my second, right?... right?

But I just knew I had to take some time this morning to hop on my computer and write this very first post before the madness begins. It's a momentous occasion, after all! (Though, who knew getting laid off and throwing all your savings into a dream boutique could be so easy?) And I firmly, firmly believe even the smallest victories deserve a celebration (preferably with bubbles).

I can't wait to celebrate all your victories with you.

See you all in only... five and a half hours. The red carpet is for YOU! And don't worry, if there's a line, we'll stay open all night. And into the next morning, if needed. I'll bring my coffee machine.

I don't even know you, and I love you all already! I will become the new best friend you didn't know you needed, the friend with all the fashion advice (I used to be a fashion writer, in case you didn't know), and the friend to make you not just look gorgeous, but feel gorgeous, too.

Oh, and my name is Ellie.

Did I not even introduce myself? How silly of me.

I'd better get some more coffee in me before I go really crazy. See you, gorgeous females on the red carpet!

Ellie x

Chapter 1: Ellie Edwards

Age: 29 years and 7 months… (Yes, not quite 30)

Relationship Status: – NEVER again…but doesn't stop me helping you with the one…or the one right now…

Opinion of Love: Always loved being in love and sharing life with someone, but since her latest heartbreak, she has sworn off love for EVER, but is looking forward to helping others find the one. Style: Classic fashion style, often referred to as timeless or traditional style, with elegance, simplicity, and sophistication.

Ellie jumped out of bed with an excitement she hadn't felt in years, ready and excited for the big launch of her new boutique. Today was the day her dream was going to come true. They say revenge is best served cold, but as far as she was concerned, revenge was best served sparkling.

Today, she was going to show them that she was over it. They could have each other; she had her dazzling, bright future out with the old and in with the new.

Exactly sixteen months ago, Ellie walked in on Jake, her boyfriend of three years, in bed with his junior assistant. And not just any bed. No, they were in the bed she bought, in the bedroom she painted, in the apartment she found for them.

But Ellie wasn't thinking of any of that today. No, today was all about positivity, new beginnings, and showing the world she'd moved on. Let karma deal with Jake.

Fifty minutes later: dress check, hair check, Valentinos check, makeup check, red lippy check and for the final touch, a spray of No. 5… check. Just on cue, the doorbell rang and Ellie heard one of her favourite voices.

"Hey Ellie, you ready, darling? Your limousine awaits. Well, your white sporty Merc, all valeted and ready to take you to your destination."

Chase was Ellie's 'older' friend (something she would never let him forget, even if it was only a matter of a few months). If it hadn't been for Chase over the past year, Ellie wouldn't be checking her reflection one last time in the mirror before a date with destiny. He was the one who picked her up after she booted Jake to the curb. He dragged her out of bed, made her dress up and show up when all she really wanted to do was snuggle under the covers and hide with a mountain of chocolate ice cream for comfort.

And that certainly wasn't the first or only time he'd gotten her through a bad breakup. Chase and Ellie met at university, and one of her earliest memories of him was Chase mopping up her tears with a Gucci pocket square on a curb outside a terrible club. They survived exams and heartbreak together through copious amounts of coffee, too many drunken nights out, and side-splitting amounts of laughter.

Chase was the kindest, flirtiest, and funniest guy you could meet. If he wasn't gay, she was sure they would have hooked up on many occasions after one too many Cosmopolitans.

It should have been a sign that Chase never liked Jake. But to Ellie, Jake did appear to have it all: a good job, a lovely family, and a great physique (the quality Ellie admittedly liked most when she first laid eyes on him). Everything came easily to him, including, apparently, cheating.

But Ellie was not thinking of any of that. Her future had a big red bow on it, and she had a giant pair of scissors with which to cut it.

"Well, how do I look?"

At the top of the stairs, Ellie gave Chase a twirl in her dress. "Exquisite darling," he said, smiling as he faked a swoon.

"Exactly how a woman should look when opening her first boutique: gorgeous, powerful, successful and, of course, with a hint of sexy."

Ellie hurried down the stairs and smacked her friend playfully with her clutch.

"You really do know how to make a girl feel good," she said. "Shall we?"

"Are you ready?" Chase asked.

Ellie had no doubts that Shoperapy would be nothing less than a smashing success. She was more ready than she'd ever been in her life.

"Let's do this."

The drive to the corner of Skyler Street was only ten minutes, but today it felt to Ellie like ten hours.

"Should we tell him to go faster?" Ellie whispered to Chase. Chase checked around the driver's shoulder.

"Darling, this is a car, not a rocket ship," he said, patting her hand affectionately.

Ellie tapped her foot impatiently, so eager she was to arrive at the grand opening.

"It feels like we're going slow," she added. Chase laughed.

"Deep breaths, my dear, deep breaths."

When they were a block away, Ellie sat up straighter and opened her compact mirror to check her makeup.

"Now, I expect we will have quite the crowd," she said in a business-like manner. "So we will need to remain poised and attentive."

"Ellie, you know—"

"We must make sure that in the madness we are still giving excellent customer service," she continued, dabbing her nose.

"Dear—"

"No matter how many people are there, we cannot look flustered and overwhelmed. We must remain—"

Chase finished her thought for her, "Poised and attentive." Ellie snapped shut her compact and smiled at her friend. "Exactly."

The car slowed, and the driver announced, "We're here."

But just as Ellie reached for the door handle, Chase stopped her. His face was kind when she turned to look at him.

"Ellie, you know I am so, so proud of you," he began. "And it's just... if this opening isn't exactly what you hoped it would be... I just want you to know it will be alright."

Ellie frowned.

"But what do you mean?"

Chase opened his mouth, then closed it. Squeezing her knee, he shook his head.

"Nothing," he said. "Forget it."

The car had driven away. Already, it was around the corner, cruising down the street across from the beach. Why did it feel like Ellie's great expectations had been left in the back seat?

Outside her brand-new boutique, Ellie turned her head in one direction. And then the other. Chase was silent beside her, scratching nervously at her neck. All that was missing, it seemed, was crickets.

"Where is everyone?" Ellie asked.

Right now, there was confusion. But it was quickly turning into panic.

"Chase?"

Ellie turned to her best friend in the world for an explanation. He had a pained grimace on his face that she supposed was an attempt at a smile. He took her hand gently into hers.

"These things take time, darling," he said. "Starting a business… it… Well, it's not always easy."

Ellie shook her head. She glanced once more towards the big red bow outside a door, but not a single soul was standing outside. "I did try to warn you," Chase said as carefully as he could. "You get a little too excited sometimes. Expect a little too much too soon."

Ellie was about to protest, but Chase put a finger to her lips. Don't make me remind you of the time you came home crying because you thought Larry was proposing when he was really just tying his shoe."

"You weren't there!" Ellie cried. "The air was positively drenched with romance."

"It was a second date, love." Ellie sighed.

"Come on," Chase said, patting her hand. "Let's still cut the ribbon. Drink the champagne. This is still a night to celebrate." Ellie went along with it all, though her disappointment was obvious when Chase insisted he take a picture of her with her big scissors.

Inside her gorgeous boutique, which cost all that was left of her savings, she blew bubbles into her bubbly glass.

"Okay, so maybe I shouldn't have expected a crowd around the block," Ellie sighed. "But no one?"

They sat side-by-side on the couch. A second later, the door opened, and Chase hopped up.

"There you are," he said. "Your very first customer!"

Ellie laughed: it was all going to be alright. But as she went, what felt like her destiny, she noticed the postman's uniform.

"I believe these are for you," he said. "Shoperapy, is that right?"

Ellie sagged back to the couch. "What is it?" Chase asked.

She handed him the stack. "Bills."

Ellie's heart was heavy as she watched the people laden with shopping bags passing outside. No one hardly even glanced into the store.

"What was I thinking?" Ellie asked. "When you get laid off from a job, you're not supposed to spend your life savings on pink chandeliers for a boutique."

Chase knocked his shoulder against hers.

"C'mon, Ellie, it's only day one," Chase said. "You're tenacious. You just need to figure out how you fit in and how to reach the women who need your help. I'm not letting you give up."

He raised the bottom of her glass so she drank down her champagne. He had the bottle right there to refill it. Together, they watched as the light faded. One woman stuck her head inside, but had pulled it right back out by the time Chase and Ellie stood.

Ellie was a little tipsy by the time it was dark.

"Maybe nobody needs help with love these days," she said with a little shrug.

Chase laughed.

"Are you crazy?" he said. "There's probably a girl in every restaurant on this block getting stood up at this very moment."

"Hmm," Ellie said.

But her mind didn't move on so quickly. An idea started to form… an idea that made her smile. An idea that made the disappointment of the evening's failure fade away.

"You're probably exactly right," Ellie said a few minutes later. Chase had forgotten what they were talking about.

"Huh?" he asked.

Ellie's heart was beating fast. She stood, and Chase stared up at her in confusion. Was this a good idea? Ellie thought about it one moment longer.

Yes!

She stuck out her hand for Chase, and he reluctantly took it. Ellie dragged him excitedly from the store, and he stumbled along behind her.

"Woman, are you mad?" he laughed. "I'm going to scuff my Gucci's!"

But Ellie was determined. More than determined. This was going to work. It had to!

She pulled Chase towards the restaurants on the block and stopped to look inside all the windows. They were packed with couples leaning in close over tea candles and glasses of Chardonnay.

Chase said, "Mind sharing with me what you are looking for?"

But right at that moment, Ellie saw it: a girl with her chin in her hand, alone at a table with a wine glass nearly empty.

She grinned as she poked her finger against the glass.

"Her."

Chapter 2: Grace Wilcox

Age: 25

Relationship Status: Grace and Tim were high school sweethearts. She put her future on hold to support him as he bounced from career idea to career idea. And then, suddenly, he up and leaves to 'discover himself' in Thailand.

Opinion of Love: Believes there is a soulmate for everyone.

Style: Girly, feminine fashion. Likes dresses, skirts, blouses, and lots of features such as laces, flounces, or ruffles. Dressing girly means wearing clothes that drape beautifully to make you feel feminine.

Sitting in the restaurant, sipping a large glass of rosé, Grace was thinking it was time to leave. She'd quite obviously been stood up. She checked her phone for about the tenth time, but still no message. She thought about messaging, Cameron, her non-date, but decided against it. There's no need to embarrass herself any more than she has already: pretty much everyone in the restaurant knew from the empty table setting across from her that she hadn't been worth showing up for. How humiliating!

But despite the social awkwardness, inside, Grace knew the truth. She was not really that disappointed. In fact, as she told her friends several times, she hadn't even wanted to go on this date in the first place.

It was really a good thing that she got stood up. Well, other than the fact that she had to pay for a glass of wine that cost half her daily wages at the ice cream shop.

As Grace waited for the bill and hoped it might just never arrive, she was surprised by a woman who breathlessly came up to her table and offered her, of all things! – a free pair of shoes at her boutique.

When Grace finally got over the shock, she asked, laughing, "But why?"

The mysterious woman in a stunning evening gown put her hands firmly on her hips and said, "Because no one deserves to be stood up."

Grace, to her own surprise, accepted this strange offer, and after paying for her drink, she followed the woman outside.

A man in a tuxedo was waiting outside. When he saw Grace's hand in the woman's, he shook his head and laughed.

"My friend," he said, "you are either crazy or brilliant." The woman stuck out her tongue.

"Why not both?"

Grace immediately liked the two, who she soon learned were called Ellie and Chase.

"Shoperapy is only a block or so away," Ellie said to Grace.

Leaning in close, Chase teased, "You're running out of time to escape."

Ellie held her head high and said, "There's nothing to escape, but a good time and fabulous shoes." "And bubbles," Chase added.

Ellie winked at Grace.

"We sort of adore bubbles," she said.

Grace supposed her luck might finally be turning around, and she hurried after the friends. As they walked, on one side Ellie told Grace all about her new shop and what it meant to her, while on the other side Chase made her laugh with his stories about his disastrous dating life. She wasn't sure who to listen to as her head twisted back and forth.

"—and that's why it's not always a bad thing to get stitches in your ass," Chase was saying as they stopped outside the glass door of a dark interior.

"Because sometimes it's a hot nurse who gets to poke you in the ass," Ellie finished for him, clearly having heard the story a million times before.

Grace giggled as Chase rolled his eyes. "Her delivery is atrocious."

Ellie ignored him as she instructed Grace to close her eyes. "Okay, keep them closed, keep them closed," Ellie said as

Chase guided her blindly inside.

Grace smelled the musky scent of new leather mixed with a hint of lavender. It smelled the way she imagined the most expensive designer stores in New York smelled, and she found herself already smiling. From behind her eyelids, the lights came on.

"Almost there… almost… okay, open them!"

Peeking one eye open and then the other, Grace was stunned. "Grace, my darling, your wardrobe awaits!" Ellie exclaimed.

Grace stood in the centre of the most beautiful boutique she had ever laid eyes on, let alone ever dared to step foot inside.

Ellie beamed at her from beside a rack of colourful dresses. "The evening is yours, all yours," she said. And then, "Chase,

you pour us girls some champagne, and we'll get started on finding the perfect 'moved on already' outfit."

"Wow, Ellie," Grace smiled as she continued to look around. "This is every girl's dream in here. I love it. A hopeful place for hopeless women."

Ellie clapped her hands together excitedly.

"Well, you're in the right place! Nothing lifts the spirits like a fabulous outfit. Here, let's play dress-up!"

She grabbed Grace's hand, pulling her towards a stunning display of dresses that seemed to shimmer under the shop lights. As they shifted through the racks, Ellie held up a vibrant red dress. "This one would look spectacular on you! Just imagine how the guy who stood you up will feel when he sees you in this."

Grace laughed.

"To be honest, I don't care much," she said with a shrug. "It was a blind date I only agreed to because my friends said I was moping around too much after Tim left for Thailand."

"I see," Ellie said as she placed the dress against Grace's small frame.

Grace touched the sequinned material. Would Tim have stayed if he'd seen her in something like this? Maybe it was her clothes. In those days, she practically lived in her ice cream shop uniform. It must have been something. Something she did that made Tim need to go 'find himself' halfway around the world. Hadn't it been enough to be her soulmate? Hadn't she been enough?

"We were high school sweethearts," Grace explained.

"You poor thing," Ellie said, tucking a strand of shoulder-length dark hair behind Grace's ear.

Chase came over with a glass of champagne.

"We were going to get married," Grace continued. "Have a dozen kids. Live in a crammed house on the beach and never get sand out of our laundry machine."

Chase grumbled, "I detest sand." Ellie rolled her eyes.

"Go on, dear."

"Tim was an artist one day, a writer another. Then a film director, a model, a fashion designer," Grace said, listing things off on her home-done manicure. "And all the while I worked at the ice cream store to support us."

Crossing his arms, Chase said, "Girl, please don't tell me you bought his ticket to Thailand?"

Grace blushed, and Chase threw his hands up in the air, inadvertently spilling his champagne.

"Is he coming back at least?" Chase asked. Grace shrugged, cheeks burning sheepishly.

"He said it wasn't up to him to decide," she said. "He said he was leaving it entirely up to the 'spirits of the universe'."

"I'm feeling faint," Chase said, dramatically fanning himself. "Alright, alright," Ellie announced to calm the situation, "here's what we're going to do: Chase, you're going to pick up this mess, because you made it. And Grace, you're going to go try on this dress, because you deserve it."

Thinking about Tim had brought down Grace's spirits a little, but Ellie's enthusiasm was contagious.

"We can give it a try, at least," she said. Ellie winked.

"That's the spirit, my dear."

Moments later, Grace emerged from the changing room, clad in the striking dress. The fabric hugged her waist perfectly and flowed like a river around her legs.

"Ta-da!" Ellie exclaimed, hands on her hips and a wide grin on her face. "You look breathtaking! Move around a bit so you can get a sense of how you feel in the dress. As well as looking good, you need to feel good, too!"

Grace twirled, the dress swirling around her and causing Ellie and Chase to clap with glee. "See? You've got to exude confidence! You're a queen, Grace. I want you to feel glorious!"

With her spirits lifted, Grace laughed, "Maybe I could conquer a few hearts in this!"

"And crush a few, too!" Ellie winked, before rummaging through more clothes.

Next, Ellie pulled out a fabulous pair of silver, high-heeled shoes and matching accessories.

"These would go perfectly! And remember, we're here to have fun. Try them on, you'll feel like a million bucks! Every girl needs a pair of killer heels to elevate her look and add a sexy touch to their outfit."

As Grace slipped into those heels, her voice suddenly high with laughter. "How do I walk in these without toppling over?"

She was used to sensible shoes fit for long shifts at the ice cream shop. Not stilettos!

"Oh, darling! Just strut like you own the catwalk!" Chase replied, mimicking a model's stance, twirling as he pretended to walk down an imaginary runway.

Grace joined in on the fun, matching Chase's exaggerated movements. "Look out, world, here comes Grace!" she declared, posing dramatically.

The laughter filled the small shop, wrapping around them like a warm blanket on a cold night. Next, Ellie produced a dazzling sequinned jacket. "You can't have a proper outfit without some bling!" She draped it over Grace's shoulders, and it sparkled under the lights.

"This is almost too much!" Grace laughed, admiring herself in the mirror.

"Too much? Never! More is more, Grace! How about we add this feathery boa?" Ellie squealed, tossing a flamboyant feather boa around Grace's neck.

The three burst into laughter, their spirits buoyed as they styled Grace to the nines. "We'll call this the Jilted Queen look!" Ellie announced, giving Grace a thumbs-up. "Now, you need to practise your best 'I've moved on' walk. Ready?"

With the shop full of energy despite it only being the three of them, Grace strutted around, practising her newly acquired 'jilted' persona, each step shedding a bit of her heartache.

"I think I'm ready to exude confidence!" she declared; arms raised like a victorious champion.

Ellie clapped with joy, "Now that's the spirit! Let's grab some photos for Instagram! You're going to make all of Meadowbank jealous!"

The three spent the rest of the night laughing, dressing up, and posing for silly pictures that captured every joyous moment. With each outfit change, Ellie encouraged Grace to speak in an over-the-top diva voice, turning the daunting experience of heartbreak into a light-hearted fashion show. With the champagne flowing, Chase took on the role of fashion commentator, making Grace feel amazing with his infectious voice and over-the-top descriptions of how Gor-ge-OUS she looked.

As midnight approaches, Grace looks at herself in yet another mirror, this time clad in an outlandishly fun ensemble complete with a sparkling tiara. It was crazy, it was bold, and most importantly, it was uplifting.

"Thank you, Ellie," Grace said, her heart feeling lighter. "Tonight, has been amazing. I never thought I could laugh so much after everything."

"Darling, that's my gift to you! Fashion is fun and healing," Ellie replied. "Remember, no one can define your worth but you. Now, let's get you this outfit — it's time to show the world your sparkle!"

As Grace stepped out of the shop, clad in her new attire and beaming with newfound confidence, she knew that while heartache was tough, it couldn't dull her sparkle.

"See you tomorrow, Ellie and Chase, and thank you so much for the invite for coffee!" she called, turning back for one last glimpse at the warm, vibrant shop filled with laughter and revitalising charm.

"Go out there and rock it, darling!" Chase shouted, waving with infectious enthusiasm, as Grace walked into the night, feeling ready to embrace whatever came next.

Grace nearly floated onto her bicycle, and she was so happy. Her helmet didn't exactly work with a tiara, but she didn't care. Her skirt flapped in the wind as she pedalled towards home, just a few blocks away.

But she was so lost in dreamy thoughts, that she completely ignored the pedestrian crossing up ahead. She saw him so late that she had to slam on her brakes, nearly toppling sideways to avoid hitting him. One of her heels came off at an abrupt stop. The asphalt was still warm from the day beneath her bare toes.

"Oh my gosh," she cried. "I am so sorry! Are you alright?"

It took a moment to push her helmet back up over her eyes after it had fallen forward. But when she did, she looked up and met the eye of a man standing petrified in the headlights from her handlebars.

He was tall, a little older, in a trench coat, Grace thought only millionaires and spies wore. His hair was neatly combed, his chin clean-shaven. This was the sort of man who drank martinis, who read newspapers, who never went to ice cream shops like the one where Grace worked. And yet there was a kindness in his eyes – no man had looked at her like that before.

Their gaze met, and neither turned away in the silence. Grace didn't know what to do. Her palms were suddenly slick on her handlebars.

"I'm sorry," she said hastily when the man opened his mouth to speak. Pushing back onto her bike, she pedalled quickly past him, saying one last time, "Really, I'm so sorry."

She was breathing so quickly, her heart pounding so noisily, that she almost couldn't make out what he called after her. But she was pretty sure it was something like this:

"Miss, you've forgotten a shoe!"

It was a good guess, because when Grace glanced down at her rapidly pedalling feet, there was the sparkly toe of a shoe on one side and a two-week-old pedicure on the other.

Chapter 3: Ellie

Ellie fell back on the velvet couch in the centre of her boutique with a satisfied sigh. It was good that the bottle of champagne was still against the cushions, because her glass was empty. There were those people who said half-empty and those who said half-full, but Ellie could be down to her very last drop and still call what she had in life full! Full to the brim!

"Lift."

Chase prodded Ellie's extended legs with the broom. He was sweeping up all the pink feathers and gold sequins that had fallen from all the boas and mini-dresses Grace had tried on for fun.

"Since when do you clean?" Ellie asked.

She tugged him down beside her on the couch and tossed away the broom. Chase accepted her glass. Ellie contented herself with the bottle. Her heart felt like it couldn't get any bigger as she tapped the bottle against Chase's glass.

"Ellie."

Oh, that was not good. Ellie knew that tone of voice. It was Chase's Mr. Responsibility' voice. Did she really need to remind him of the time in college when he bought a vintage Valentino belt instead of groceries? She fed him instant Ramen for two weeks straight. His veins were probably still clearing out.

"Ellie," Chase repeated when she rolled her eyes. "We're celebrating, dear friend," she said.

"You know I don't like to be this person," he said. "I much prefer to be the 'order three servings of blueberry pancakes from the most expensive brunch in town and worry about paying for it later' kind of guy."

"Then be that guy," Ellie said. Chase sighed.

"It's just that, you know," he said, laying his hand over Ellie's leg. "We didn't technically make a sale."

"Grace left with a whole outfit!" Ellie protested.

"And while she looked absolutely divine," Chase said. "That's technically a loss."

Ellie huffed in protest and crossed her arms defiantly.

"A young woman going out into the world after being stood up, feeling beautiful and strong and confident, is no loss in my book," Ellie argued.

Chase shook his head with a little chuckle and emptied his glass. With a small smile, Ellie turned to her friend. He met her eye and raised a perfectly shaped eyebrow. She sighed and lay her cheek against his shoulder.

"Don't worry," she said. "I know."

Chase patted Ellie's leg and rested his cheek against her head. "You'll figure it out, love," he said.

She nodded. She knew she would. In fact, she knew she would do anything to make it so.

The two best friends spent a quiet moment together, enjoying each other's company, dreaming of what the future could hold.

After a while, Chase said, "Girl, you better not be getting blush on my silk jacket."

Ellie laughed and swatted at Chase's arm as she raised herself back up. Chase stood and, after a big stretch and an even bigger yawn, offered his hand. Ellie smiled, but shook her head.

"I'm going to stay a little longer, I think," she said. Chase gave her a concerned look, which made Ellie laugh.

"I'm happy, darling," she said. "Even if my accountant isn't, I am. Tonight was a great success."

Chase grinned at her. He leaned over and kissed her forehead. "Alright, my dear," he said. "Enjoy your success. But don't stay too late, alright? Beauty sleep and all that." Ellie laughed.

"Some need it more than others, darling."

Chase mocked a grave insult, hand against his heart, mouth open.

"I obviously wasn't talking about you, Casanova," Ellie joked.

Chase narrowed his eyes at her playfully. He pointed a nicely manicured finger.

"You better not have been," he said.

They both broke into laughter a second later. Chase gathered up his things and, after one last kiss on Ellie's cheek, headed towards the door of Shoperapy. He paused halfway through the glass door.

"Are you sure you're alright, Ellie Bug?" he asked, watching her carefully.

Ellie nestled deeper into the cushions and smiled contentedly as she stretched her arms overhead. Sighing and settling back down like a sleepy cat, she nodded.

"My dear friend, so far this has been the best night of my life," she replied.

This made Chase smile.

"Well, I hope it continues to be," he said. Ellie grinned.

"I don't know how it possibly couldn't."

Chase winked and slipped out into the night, which was balmy and warm beneath patio lights strung across the quaint shopping street. Ellie rose only to turn off the main shop lights, leaving just the soft pink light of a few antique lamps with adorable tassels. Then she settled back in, happy to think over the events of the day.

Opening Day.

You only get one. Not like a wedding. Not like a divorce, even. And while hers hadn't been exactly as she'd imagined it that morning or all the mornings which stretched back months and months, it had, in its own way, been perfect. When she told her great-great grandchildren about this one day (adopted, of course, because her family will fore-sworn of love thanks to her wisdom), they'd hear about Grace's laughter, the sequins and feathers all over the floor like confetti, and this moment right here, Ellie contented and satisfied in solitude.

She was enjoying her reflections and daydreams about the future when her peace was interrupted by a man stalking to the front door, wrenching it open, and storming inside. Ellie had been secretly wishing for another customer the whole time, even when she was more than happy to just help Grace. But something about this man huffing and puffing and glaring told her that he may not be there for a cashmere scarf at half past 11. Still, Ellie had read on an online blog about starting your own business that it was good policy to treat everyone like a potential customer.

"Good evening," she said, standing up and hiding her champagne bottle behind her back, "Welcome to Shoperapy, where the clothes aren't just for your body, but your heart."

The man had been advancing angrily towards Ellie, a whole string of words on his tongue. But he stopped mid-stride. For a moment, it didn't seem he could say a word as Ellie smiled politely, expectantly. He shook his head.

"What did you say?" he asked.

His voice was prickly like a wool sweater, admittedly, a gorgeous wool sweater.

Smiling, Ellie began again, "Good evening. Welcome to—" "I'm not here to shop," the man interrupted.

He laughed a little. Bitterly. Irritated. But still, there was something of amusement in front of him as he eyed Ellie, seeing her differently than before.

"Does it look like I'm here to shop?" he asked, sweeping his hands over his body.

Ellie didn't need an excuse to look. The man was tall, fit, handsome as the devil in a slim-fit suit jacket. Sure, his narrow blue tie was askew, clearly tugged loose in some kind of distress. But it matched his deep, dark eyes. And even if those eyes flashed with irritation, it didn't change the fact that Ellie very much liked them. Oysters would probably glare at her, too, if they could before she plopped them hungrily into her mouth.

"Well?" the man pressed.

Feeling her own irritation at the man's rudeness, Ellie said begrudgingly, "I suppose you don't match my exact target demographic." With a tilt of her head, she added, "A bit too... sweaty."

The man—no, the intruder—wiped roughly at his brow. It was a nice brow, Ellie had to admit. "You ruined my night," he said.

Ellie frowned. Then laughed. Then crossed her arms. "I ruined your night?" she asked.

Was he not the one who stormed in right when she was in the middle of a very nice moment with herself and her dreams?

"That's right," he said stubbornly. "That's exactly right and you know it."

Ellie would have been gracious if this man, who clearly had made some mistake, had been at least the tiniest bit humble or shown just a fraction of, you know, basic human kindness. But that was not the case. And so Ellie felt no guilt about getting all riled up herself.

She found herself stepping closer to this annoyingly hot donkey's you-know-what. She hadn't really meant to. But there she was. Admiring his cologne and trying to remain disgusted. "I didn't ask you to come barrelling in here like a bull in a

China shop," she said.

The man grinned wickedly as he leaned in towards her and said, "And I didn't ask you to come convince my date to leave the restaurant I'd booked three weeks in advance."

Realisation struck Ellie like a freight train. She put her hand to her mouth as she stared up at the man in shock.

With even more anger boiling up in her chest, Ellie said, pointing,

"You're the stand-up-er!"

The man's confusion competed with his irritation.

"The 'stand-up-er'? That's not a— you know what, never mind. My name is Cameron Kelly, and I didn't deserve what you so arrogantly did to me tonight."

Ellie was even more stunned.

"Arrogant? Me?" she stammered. "You, Mr. Kelly, are the one who got a young woman's hopes up for a romantic evening, for perhaps a love-at-first-sight story. And you, Stand up-er, yes, Stand up-er, are the one who so cruelly decided that you just couldn't be bothered. I don't think there's any doubt here as to who the arrogant one is, sir."

Cameron, or whatever his dumb name was, laughed spitefully. "I was fifteen minutes late, because I was helping one of my elderly clients at the gym, and it took a little longer than usual. I work across the street, you know. That's where I was when you were dragging a poor woman to this-this-this explosion of tackiness!"

Ellie had to clutch her chest. She had to reach out to catch herself from falling on a glass side table. Vintage, she might add. And the definition of class.

"First of all," she said, voice shaking, "one does not down a double pour of rose in 'fifteen minutes'. So, please, come up with a better lie next time." Ellie recovered enough to stand, to smooth down her dress, to lift her chin defiantly towards Cameron. "Second of all, you and your polyester tie, which is the only reason your eyes look so blue probably, wouldn't know class and elegance and fashion if it hit you in your, I'm sure, very toned ass."

Did Ellie imagine it, or did Cameron's mouth twitch towards a smile? It didn't matter, she thought as she shouldered past him towards the door of her shop. It didn't matter if he smiled. She didn't care at all what he looked like. Whether he had cute dimples or not. Whether he had a little gap between his front teeth. Or if he bit his lower lip as he grinned at her... No, she didn't care about any of that.

Ellie gripped the door handle firmly and pulled it with hot blood pumping through her veins.

"And third of all—"

"Let me guess," Cameron interrupted. He turned and began walking towards her. He stopped right in front of her. Not even the cool of the night breeze could take away the heat that suddenly flooded Ellie's cheeks as he leaned in close and said, "Get lost?"

Ellie glared up at him, trying not to count the number of blues she could see in his eyes.

"No," she said.

He was somehow even cuter when he arched his eyebrow and looked down at her mischievously. And why did he have to smell so darn good?

"No?" he said.

Ellie just jutted her chin up at him.

"No, that's not what I was going to say at all," she said. Cameron grinned as if to say, 'Well, go on then.'

"I was going to say," she said, "Get lost and never come back."

Cameron laughed. Ellie immediately wanted to hear that sound again.

"Excuse me," Cameron said. "That is clearly very different from what I guessed."

Ellie nodded, heart beating powerfully.

Tilting his head, Cameron said, "Evening, Ms. Unreasonable."
"Good evening, Mr. Stand-up-er."

She slammed the door shut behind him. She flipped the sign quickly to 'Closed'. Then she pressed her back against the door. Her palms were hot against the cool glass.

What was that?

Ellie tried to breathe in evenly to steady herself. It was really nothing. Nothing at all. She'd stood up for Grace. She'd put a man in his place when his charming smile had probably let him skate by with all kinds of reprehensible behaviour throughout his life. She hadn't backed down.

It was over. It was nothing.

And, most importantly of all, she was done with love. With wildly beating hearts. With instant connections. With that strange smile that wouldn't leave the lips.

She'd sworn it off. For good this time. So it was nothing.

Ellie said to herself, "Nothing. No, nothing at all."

> ## SHOE FOUND!!!
>
> To the very charming woman with eyes like diamonds who had me like a deer in the headlights in front of her bicycle, I retrieved your silver shoe.
>
> How do I find you?
>
> I'd like to return what was lost.
>
> I'd like to see you again.
>
> You didn't hit me, but I am, nonetheless, struck.
>
> Can anyone please help me?

Posted: June 10th, 2025; 9:29 PM (GMT)

User: Your Fashion Ellie-vator

Subscribers: 23

Hello, you gorgeous humans, I hope you're all having as exciting a time as me. Shoperapy has now been open for almost a week, and while perhaps I'm not yet 'rolling in the dough', it is so far wildly successful in 'raking in the love'.

Only the other night, a very sweet gentleman came in with a silver shoe, asking me if it was perhaps purchased at my boutique. He was so stricken by the woman who had lost it (after apparently nearly knocking him over with her bicycle) that he just had to find her. Oh, the romance. Oh, the intrigue!

And of course, I know who the gorgeous female wielding the near-deadly bicycle is. What a twist of fate that she works in the icecream shop only a few doors down. Do you all feel the start of a love story, or is it just me?

I, for one, am so excited to be part of a budding romance. Or at least what I hope is one. I'm fairly sure the woman in question will be ecstatic when she's reunited with her Prince Charming… However, there is still a Prince Not-So-Charming somewhat in the picture. Hmm. Things could get interesting, my lovelies.

Keep following and, of course, share with friends, and I will keep you updated when Prince Charming returns the shoe. And when our beautiful Cinderella accepts it.

Or darts out to escape on her bicycle… See you all in Shoperapy very soon,

Ellie x

Chapter 4: Jess Olsen

Age: 35

Relationship Status: She's had a crush on her coworker Adam since the day she met him, but so far, they've only been super close friends and nothing more.

Opinion of Love: Loves the idea of dating and the idea of love, even though she's never really been in love.

Style: Bohemian fashion. Maxi dresses and flats, which give you a romantic edge.

Jess was pretty sure that she'd been in that section before. She reached out and touched a silky purple blouse. She was pretty sure she'd seen it an hour earlier. But it was all beginning to look the same. The long racks are stuffed with clothes. The white plastic, headless mannequins are pointing this way and that. The lighting was both too bright and too dim. Finger to her chin, she spun around, searching for something to help her find her way. She'd heard of hikers getting lost just like this — not that Jess was much for nature. She was a workaholic civil engineer, so the closest she got to the forest was at the office's monstrous printer as it shot out dozens upon dozens of sheets.

But in the few spare moments for herself she had, Jess occasionally watched those shows where people are dropped in the middle of nowhere, sometimes naked, sometimes not, sometimes with their ex, sometimes with a stranger, sometimes with the goal of creating drama, sometimes just to survive. So Jess knew the signs well enough - exhaustion, confusion, dehydration, the beginning of hallucinations.

She didn't need to fly to the Amazon when she had it all right there: the jungle that was the Big Department Store.

Just to catch her breath and sit for a moment or two, Jess ducked inside the nearest dressing room. She plopped down under her armful of outfits. She couldn't even remember picking up half of them. Were they even her size? Was a wool sweater insane for early summer? What was she thinking?

Jess was as sharp as a whip, but the second she stepped inside that perfumed, air-conditioned maze…

With a defeated sigh, Jess leaned her head back against the partition of the dressing room stall. She'd mistakenly thought she had passed the hard part: getting her long-time friend and coworker to ask her out on a date. But that was years and years of longing, waiting, misunderstanding, crying, despairing, hoping, and swearing off the chance again and again, and it felt now like the snap of the fingers compared to finding something to wear.

A knock at her dressing room door interrupted Jess from what was quickly turning into an unexpected nap. She sat up straighter, even though no one could see her.

"Ma'am?" came a man's voice. "Can I get you any different sizes? How are things looking?"

Jess glanced down at the bundle of clothes in her arms. She had half a mind to be completely honest and answer, 'Crumpled'. But instead, she began to kick off her shoes and called out, "Still giving everything a try."

The store attendant's voice was friendly, almost sympathetic, Jess thought, as he replied, "No problem, hun. Take your time. I'm here if you need anything."

Jess's shoulders slumped as he walked away. Anything? More like everything. She needed the confidence to tell Adam she wanted more, she needed the faith to believe he could feel the same way about her that she'd always felt about him, she needed calm to survive the next few days till the date. Oh, and she needed something to wear, because it would really be sending too strong a signal if she showed up naked.

Jess pulled each item of clothing from its hanger with a bewildered look. Had she really chosen this? Was it possible she'd accidentally switched her mountain of clothes with another woman's mountain of clothes?

And it only got worse when she started trying things on.

She was uncertain about everything. Was that blue too blue? Did that cardigan itch, or was it just her being sensitive? Was a tight dress too forward? Was the loose-fitting trouser not forward enough? Would he get scared off if she wore a dress with flowers, which might remind him of bouquets, which might remind him of weddings, which might remind him he's really too young to be settling down, especially with his best friend?

Did they really want to ruin what they had going? Was a different kind of love really worth risking no love at all?

It was in that moment, in a totally wrong dress half unzipped, that it hit Jess that perhaps her uncertainty about what to wear had something to do with her uncertainty about where she and Adam stood. How could she know which blouse to pick when she wasn't entirely sure whether it was a date or a date-date? Did he see this as more the way she did?

Jess chewed at her fingernails, a bad habit she developed during her final exams in college. She wouldn't know the answer to her questions till she was walking into the cute little restaurant he'd picked for them, wearing… wearing… oh, wearing what?

"How's it going in there?"

The store attendant was back. Jess cleared her throat, which had been seconds away from a desperate sob.

Still, her voice was uncertain as she said, "Umm, it's alright." "Can I clear anything out of the room for you?" he asked.

Jess looked around at the mess. An explosion beneath horrible fluorescent lights. A massacre of rejected outfits. It was gruesome.

"Sure," Jess replied, "just give me a second."

She gathered everything up into her arms — every piece of item down to the thin sequin scarf she'd been crazy to think would work for a date/date-date. When she opened the dressing room door, the store attendant's eyes went wide. It was as if an avalanche was coming towards him. In many ways, one was. Stumbling back beneath the weight of the discarded clothes, the employee happened to catch a look at Jess's distraught face.

"Having a tough time finding something?" he asked.

Jess could only nod. She was afraid that if she started speaking, she'd also start crying.

"Hold on," the man said.

He went up the row of dressing rooms. He checked out of the store, looking back and forth several times. Jess had her head out of her own room, watching with curiosity.

A moment later, the man turned back around, tossed all the clothes into a dressing room, and slammed shut the door. He hurried towards Jess and held out his hand.

"Come with me," he said.

Jess just stared. What in the world was going on?

"Trust me," he said, smiling a brilliant smile. "I know where you'll find what you're looking for, for both your figure and your heart."

Jess laughed. This was ridiculous. She didn't know this man. And didn't he work here? There's no way he was supposed to be taking her somewhere else.

And yet, there was something about the man. And without really thinking about it, Jess found herself reaching for the man's hand. Just when she was about to touch her fingers to his, she hesitated.

"Wait, I'm still in this dress!"

The man noticed and then said, "Spin." "Spin?"

"Spin, spin, darling."

Jess spun. With a deft hand, the man zipped her up. A second later, he was back with a pair of shoes.

"A five?"

Jess hardly had time to answer. He was slipping her foot into the heel as if he'd done it a million times. Then he closed the door on her old sweats (the only clothes she owned besides suits for work) and her dingy old trainers. They moved like spies through the department store, ducking here and there behind displays and racks of clothes.

"I'm Chase, by the way," the man said when they hid amongst

some evening gowns halfway through the store.

Jess giggled like she'd just made a new friend as a kid. Or maybe it was the feathers on one of the gowns tickling her nose. "Jess," she said.

Chase grinned.

"Coast's clear," he said and took her hand.

"We're going outside?" Jess asked as he held open the door for her.

She once again doubted whether she'd made the right decision to go on this wild adventure. It took her years to hint at a date-date dinner with Adam. Jess was not a risk taker, a big leaper, or a no-looker.

But Chase laughed as they darted across the street through traffic, and so she laughed too. A few blocks down the way, stumbling all along in her heels, Jess came to a stop when Chase came to a stop. Just ahead, Jess could see the shimmer of the sea beneath the bright blue skies.

Chase took a moment to tidy himself. He wiped his brow. Straightened his lapels. Smiled graciously as he bowed and swept open a door Jess had hardly taken into account. Thanking Chase, she stepped inside a beautiful boutique.

It smelled lovely (not overpowering like the mall), the light was natural and soft, and it was quiet amongst the thoughtful display of curated clothes. Jess smiled knowingly at Chase.

Yes, this had been the right decision. Definitely the right decision to just trust herself and go.

A woman in a gorgeous cream laced matching set emerged from behind the checkout counter and swept like a sunrise cloud towards Jess to greet her. Jess immediately knew she was in good hands. And she didn't even know the woman's name.

"Ellie, dear," Chase said, "mind bringing back Jess's dress and shoes when she's done? We both know you'll find her something infinitely better."

Jess grinned over her shoulder at Chase, who winked and, with a little wave, ran off back towards work.

Ellie. He'd said the woman's name was Ellie.

Ellie was going to find her something to wear, and it would all work out.

Ellie.

She'd have to remember the name when she was writing the speech for her engagement party with Adam...

Posted: 9:31 PM (GMT)

User: Your Fashion Ellie-vator

Subscribers: 19

Who Needs to Roll in the Dough, When You Can Rake in the Love; Or How I Turned Zero Sales into a Million Big Ones

Good evening, my fabulously fabulous followers! (Yes, I see each and every one of you, 19. You are all unique as a snowflake, as dazzling as a diamond.)

I am both happy and sad to report that I may have slightly underestimated how hard it was to start a business. Sad, because the rent on Shoperapy is very much real, even if my illusions are not. But happy, because while there's nothing but cobwebs in my cash box, my heart is simply overflowing. And I'll tell you why!

Just the other night, a very sweet gentleman came into my boutique (as opposed to the very rude, horrible, not even handsome at all gentleman who stormed earlier – but that, dear readers, is a story for another time...). What did he have in his hand, but a silver shoe? A silver shoe I knew like the back of my hand, because not only did I stock that silver shoe in my store, but I'd only just moments ago before given it as a gift to a lovely woman who needed a shimmery pick me up (my dear friends – you can always come to me for a pick me up, know that!).

He asked if I'd perhaps sold this to a young lady. A 'beautiful young lady' he happened to say. 'A beautiful young lady who didn't succeed in running him over, but did succeed in stealing his heart' were his exact words, if I remember correctly.

I told him, 'No,' I hadn't sold that to a young lady. He was crestfallen till I corrected, 'I'd given it to a young lady.'

Needless to say, I pointed him in the right direction because that's what I opened Shoperapy for: to point love in the right direction, whether that's towards a divine denim jumpsuit or true love's kiss.

Ladies, as I sign off for the evening, I'm well aware that I'll need to step up actual sales to keep my business afloat. But I'll sleep well enough for now, knowing that love is in the air.

Ellie x

Chapter 5: Grace Wilcox

The pretty golden light of early evening filled the ice cream shop along the boardwalk like rich caramel syrup.

Behind the glass display, Grace was trying not to be impatient as a cute little girl counted her change from the many pink-stitched pockets of her cute little overalls.

The little girl's mum, who held two dripping ice cream cones, kept smiling apologetically at Grace as her daughter kept pulling more and more pennies from her pockets.

"Is that enough?" the little girl asked her mum, pigtails swinging as she lifted her dimpled chin.

Grace almost jumped in and said, 'Close enough!' but her boss was watching. So all she could do was force a smile as her mum said with a pained glance at Grace, "Almost."

Grace told herself not to tap her toe. Be kind, she told herself. Be polite. But all she really wanted to do was check her phone. It was burning a hole in her pocket – she was sure.

She could have sworn she felt it vibrate in her apron while she was scooping the little girl's Strawberry Delight – could it finally be him?

The thought that it might be him, after all this time of waiting, waiting, dying, made Grace's heart race. She had to know. She just had to. But she had a customer. And her customer just happened to be little and adorable and blissfully unaware of boys who promise forever and leave you with 'maybe in a few months.'

Grace felt sure that it was him this time (not her mum, not her student loan lender, not a telemarketer selling timeshares in Tenerife...). So, to gently speed things along, she encouraged the little girl, "You're doing a great job. Why don't I help you with little stacks of five?"

The little girl smiled shyly, and for a moment, Grace saw herself. She remembered a grainy photo her mum used to show her: braces, a giant backpack, a nervous smile half hidden in the shoulder of a freckle-faced boy with green eyes who grinned daringly at the camera. Tim had always said she was too shy. Too quiet. Too sweet.

Despite her impatience, Grace told herself to slow down. Delicate flowers can't be crushed, after all. More coins rattled against the counter as the ice cream melted, and Grace just said, "Keep going. You're just fine."

The little girl waved to Grace as she left the store with her mum's hand in hers, ice cream already on her nose.

Grace waved, too, but the second they were out of the ice cream shop, Grace pulled her phone out. She was so excited she nearly dropped it into the Orange Creamsicle sorbet. Her heart raced. A smile tugged at her lips.

It had to be Tim, finally coming to his senses about their love, their fated-in-the-stars, once-in-a-lifetime love. They were soulmates! He'd only needed to remember. And now he had. He was texting to tell her he's coming home. Her fingers shook as she unlocked her phone and...

Nothing. Absolutely nothing.

No text message from Tim. In fact, there was no message at all. She must have completely imagined the vibration of her phone.

Did she want Tim to write to her so badly that she had started imagining things?

Was that normal? Did she need to see a doctor? With the back of her hand, Grace felt her forehead over her uniform cap. Was that how you could tell if you were going crazy? She didn't know. Grace was so hyper-focused on her phone behind the ice cream counter that, for a minute, she forgot she was at work. She was in Thailand. Some jungle. Watching Tim at a picnic table beside a shaved ice cart. Watching Tim text everyone but her.

She was so focused on the blank space on her phone where there was supposed to be a message that made it all better again that she didn't hear the little bell above the door announcing a new customer.

Nor did she hear footsteps coming towards her as she checked her conversation history with Tim. Her stomach dropped: the last thing he'd sent her was a photo of him holding Tree Pose at a temple in Chiang Mai with the message: Feeling such inner peace, you have no idea, dude.

Grace didn't hear a soft clearing of a throat on the other side of the counter. She was too busy deciding if she wanted to cry or laugh or scream. 'Dude'? Since when was she, the love of his life, his soulmate, his one and only, 'dude'? He obviously meant to send this to one of his friends. Or sent the same text to everyone in his contacts. Surely, there was no way he would call her 'dude'.

Grace didn't hear everything else before. But Grace did hear her boss shouting at her.

"Grace, you have a customer!"

She jumped and was lucky her phone fell safely back into her apron pocket. Looking up, startled, Grace found her customer smiling a little awkwardly at her. Grace was supposed to greet all customers with a loud, friendly, 'Welcome to The Three Little Scoops. Can I scoop you up something just right today?' Normally, it came like clockwork. But as she stared at the customer in front of her, she found she couldn't say a word.

It was the man from the other night. The one she nearly ran over with her bicycle. The one she ran away from.

When Grace's boss cleared his throat, Grace started talking. But so did the man from the other night.

"Welcome to The—"

"I didn't mean to get you—"

They both so happened to stop at the same time, too. And laugh embarrassingly at the same time, too.

"You go first," the man said.

Grace shook her head.

"You're the customer, you go first."

The man scratched the back of his neck. Was he shy like Grace? Grace found herself smiling.

"Well," he said, leaning in with a glance towards her boss, who had his arms crossed, "I wanted to say that I didn't mean to get you in trouble. I have one more thing to say, but you say your thing first."

Grace giggled at his over-politeness till her boss cleared his throat again.

"Alright," Grace said and stood up straighter. "Here's what I was going to say: 'Welcome to The Three Scoops. Can I scoop you up something just right today?'"

The man smiled, clearly holding back laughter. This made Grace want to laugh.

"Should I answer that, or should I say my second thing?" the man asked.

"I don't see you scooping, Grace," her boss said. "Maybe answer first," Grace said.

The man winked, which made butterflies flutter in Grace's stomach as he clasped his hands behind his back and peered at the selection of ice creams.

"Which is your favourite?" he asked softly, keeping his eyes down.

Grace pointed at one. The man nodded. "I'll take that."

Grace went to scoop the rich, velvety mint chocolate into a cone, the familiar motion reminding her of countless encounters with customers before. But when she reached for the mint, she found it slightly frozen, requiring a more forceful scoop than usual. She began to really give it some muscle when the man pulled something from his satchel and set it on the counter. She was so surprised that when the scooper popped loose, she lost her grip, and it went clattering to the floor behind her.

"Grace!"

"Sorry, Boss," Grace cried, tossing the scooper into the sink. "Your shoe," the man said, again red-cheeked from having once more gotten Grace into trouble.

Grace looked at the shoe and could not believe he was returning it. But her boss was getting impatient, so Grace held up a cone and a cup. The man pointed to the cone. And when he handed her back her shoe, Grace handed him a cone, an empty one.

Her boss chastised her: "Where is your head?"

But Grace told him she would get it together. But the man was watching her so intently, with such a sweet, amused smile on his lips, that it flustered her so much as to almost put a scoop in the shoe he'd just handed her.

"That's not right," she mumbled.

"What a disaster," her boss mumbled, too.

There was an awkward moment then of Grace trying to figure out exactly where to put her returned shoe. It wasn't ideal, but in the end, it went into her apron pocket. Her boss sighed. At least she didn't put it in the buckets of ice cream.

But when the ice cream fell out of the scoop and onto the floor, her boss finally stepped in.

"Please, excuse me, sir," he said. "This employee was just leaving to clean the bathrooms.'

The man looked at Grace with a reassuring smile, which only made her feel even more embarrassed.

Sheepishly, Grace excused herself. She didn't even remember to thank him for returning her shoe as she hurried to hide in the bathroom. Leaning against the door, she waited till her heart stopped pounding before checking through the crack in the door. The man waited a few minutes, slowly licking his mint chocolate chip ice cream cone. He kept glancing towards where Grace was hiding — or working, supposedly — though really, spying. Grace didn't even know his name. She'd been far too nervous to ask, and he'd been too shy to give it. Grace watched him in secret, finding herself smiling. But then, with one last look towards the bathroom, he left.

As the door jangled shut behind him, the silence of the shop returned, but it felt different. Grace's thoughts spiralled inward, replaying the moment over and over. She breathed deeply, trying not to think about the awkwardness of their second interaction, but it continued to linger.

She poked her head out of the bathroom. Her boss was cleaning the scoop which had fallen on the floor.

"Something tells me those bathrooms aren't spotless," her boss said.

Grace sighed and came out.

"I'm sorry, Boss," she said. "I don't know what's wrong with me today."

Was she really such a mess since Tim left, not able to do the job she could normally do in her sleep, or worse… not able to talk to men? Not even kind, respectful, handsome ones?

The thought gnawed at her, twisting her stomach into knots more complex than she had thought possible.

As her shift went on, her work at the ice cream shop continued to be disrupted by this one encounter, and that didn't sit well with her. How could this man unravel her day? And what was it that really unsettled her?

It was awkward, sure. But this was really the truth: this man, whose name she didn't even know, was kind. And Tim was... not.

And yet it was Tim who she longed to be the one to walk through the door of the ice cream shop.

Grace started to think back on their relationship... was Tim really the love of her life, her soulmate? They spoke of a future together, filled with adventures and shared dreams, as if the universe had conspired to bring them together. Or had she just imagined this, like she imagined her phone vibrating?

Grace could still remember the day when he said those painful words, his voice steady yet cold, like an icy wind cutting through her dreams. 'I'm going to Thailand,' he had declared. Those four words shattered her illusions, echoing in her mind like a haunting refrain. He didn't even ask her if she wanted to go... Looking back now, she realised that perhaps she had been blinded by hope, mistaking infatuation for true love. She was starting to think Tim was not her soulmate; he was a lesson filled with heartache. A part of her wished she could forget she ever knew Tim, as the heartache was too much at times. The memories of their past reminded her of the void left behind.

As the sunlight dipped below the horizon, casting long shadows across the park, Grace understood that she had to let go. It was time to turn the page and embrace the future, no longer ensnared by a fleeting romance that had promised a forever but delivered only longing... but she couldn't.

She read his last text again. He hadn't asked about her; he hadn't said he missed her. And yet, after three months, Grace still believed Tim would come back. What was wrong with her?

Her boss was suddenly at her side, holding out a clean ice cream scooper.

"I ran it under hot water," she said. "Helps when things are stuck."

Her boss was hard on her, but, at the end of the day, always fair and kind.

"For matters of the heart," he added, giving Grace a confident look, "I don't have such an easy answer... but distracting yourself helps. Say, with serving ice cream?"

Grace smiled and took the scooper.

As she returned to her duties, Grace resolved to shake off the feeling that had threatened to consume her. With every scoop she prepared, she found a renewed sense of purpose. After all, there were many wonderful customers to serve, and, in time, the feelings of her encounter with the man with the shoe would disappear. It's not like she would ever see him again... or would she?

The queue in front of her lengthened – the busiest part of the day. Teenagers engaged in spirited debates over which flavours to choose, their voices forming a delightful sound against the backdrop of Grace's now cheerful repartee.

Nearby, a young father clutched his daughter's tiny hand, her eyes wide with wonder as she excitedly pointed to the rainbow-swirled tub of bubble-gum ice cream. At the same time, elderly couples exchanged knowing smiles, their soft chuckles laced with nostalgia for summers long past, where ice cream held a sacred place in their hearts.

Just then, the bell sounded again as a new wave of customers appeared, a lively group of friends enjoying a summer outing. Their carefree laughter enveloped the shop, mixing with the melodic sound of music drifting from the speakers. They crowded around the counter, immersed in spirited discussions and playful banter, while Grace cheerfully responded to their whims, dishing up cones piled high with indulgent combinations.

Outside, the world spun relentlessly onward. Yet, within the comforting confines of the ice cream shop, time seemed to suspend itself, transforming the very air into an excitement of happiness.

Grace often paused to glance out the window, not sure who she was looking for any more…

At the end of her shift, Grace was relieved the rest of her day had gone by without too much excitement, and she headed to get her bag… her favourite pink one. The perfect size, the perfect colour!

She hung her apron on the hook in the back and reached in to pull something from the big front pockets. But this time, it wasn't her phone she wanted to see. It was the shoe.

G OMG, a man has just returned my shoe!

E Oh, that is fab. I told him to go to The Three Scoops. He was insistent he return it to you himself.

G Don't know what came over me, but I was so flustered I could hardly serve him.

E Maybe because he was VERY charming?

G Haha, he was charming! But I wish I'd been more confident self.

E I'm sure he loved you just for you.

G Clumsy and shy and awkward?

E And sweet and lovely and kind.

G Thanks, Ellie. I needed to hear that.

E Anytime, my girl x

Chapter 6: Ellie

Ellie was heading to bed for an early night when her phone beeped. She was so glad Grace had got her shoe back and even more glad she felt flustered by the charming man. Ellie's mind went into overdrive. Maybe this was a sign Grace was getting over Tim, and the beginning of a new romance... it was so sweet to have such sweet dreams.

The next morning, Ellie woke early. Being so preoccupied with the shop, she hadn't been following her usual morning ritual. She knew she had to get back on track – so her alarm was set early. And she was not going to snooze.

As the sunrise cast a golden hue over her cottage, illuminating the world like a soft spotlight on a grand stage, Ellie's eyes fluttered open to the symphony of birdsong outside her window. A profound sense of anticipation washed over her, invigorating her spirit. Ellie stretched luxuriously, feeling the comforting weight of her duvet as it reluctantly released her into the day. Her bare feet met the cool wooden floorboards, the sudden chill sending a jolt through her senses and signalling the commencement of a day filled with promise.

Today was the day she was going to make those sales.

The bathroom beckoned, its pristine tiles reflecting the first light of dawn. Ellie splashed her face with cool water, feeling it cascade over her skin like a fresh morning dew. Gazing into the mirror, Ellie looked at the determination sparkling in her eyes. It was a new day full of potential at the boutique. She only needed to seize it.

After the dutiful stuff (teeth, floss, deodorant), it was time for the fun stuff: the 'Choosing of the Outfit'.

Ellie's wardrobe was a mini version of Shoperapy: a treasure trove filled with garments that told tales of her worldwide journeys. Each piece, carefully selected over countless shopping adventures, resonated with memories. Deciding on what to wear was like deciding on a favourite photo in a beloved album: very, very difficult.

After much contemplation, Ellie settled on a chic navy dress adorned with delicate white polka dots. She felt it reflected her personality that day —playful yet sophisticated, with a hint of whimsy. Accessorising it with a statement belt to accentuate her figure, Ellie felt an unwavering confidence to embrace whatever challenges the day may present. And if the last few days were anything to go by, she knew there would be more than a few. Challenges, that is. A navy tote bag from Valentino, a birthday gift from Chase, completed her outfit before heading to the kitchen for her first meal of the day.

Breakfast was scones and tea: the perfect energiser for a bustling, but successful day ahead. Then Ellie gathered her everyday essentials (phone, purse, keys, red Chanel lipstick), put on her red Marc Jacob sunglasses, and headed out to a day she'd manifested to perfection.

There was an invigorating kiss to the crisp morning air. The town buzzed with an energetic rhythm. As Ellie made her way to Shoperapy (where she would sell something that day!), each step pulsed with eagerness and anticipation. She greeted the familiar faces of shop owners as she passed by, their cheerful greetings creating a sense of camaraderie.

Finally, she arrived at her storefront, its polished windows gleaming like jewels in the sunlight. Everything was perfect from the outside: an elegant display of the latest collection, creative touches here and there, and little winks to discerning customers. How could some fashionable lady not want to step inside? It was beyond welcoming. It was—

WARNING: DO NOT SHOP HERE.

THE OWNER IS STUBBORN, UNYIELDING, AND INSUFFERABLE. SHE MAY BE CUTE, BUT DON'T BE FOOLED. SHE IS A PORCUPINE.

– SIGNED, THE STUNG

Ellie pushed her sunglasses up onto the top of her head as if that is the problem: her eyesight. But no. The sign still said the same thing as she squinted in the morning sunshine. And she still couldn't believe it.

With a huff, Ellie tore down the sign 'someone' had taped up to the front door of her shop and stormed inside. She balled up the sign as tightly as she could, liking how it felt to squeeze it smaller and smaller. And then she tossed it directly into the trash.

Ellie had spent the morning prioritising positivity, sending good vibes out into the universe, and loving herself so that she could love others. But just like that, she felt like she'd been dragged out of bed after a night of tequila shots to show up for jury duty in scratchy wool pants.

"It's fine," she muttered to herself behind her cash register. "I'm fine."

She knew exactly who put it up, of course. What nerve he had! To call himself 'The Stung'. Ellie laughed out loud. Literally. 'The Stung.' Please. She was going to need to go to the eye doctor if she kept rolling her eyes that hard.

He stood Grace up. And came up with the lamest excuse why. 'The Stung.'

More like 'The Stinger!'

Ellie was glad she stood up to him. Yes, she was. Someone needed to. And she was happy it was her. She nodded her chin even though she was the only one in the shop. Yes, she did the right thing. She would not let dating bullies just wander the streets freely, never facing any consequences.

But as Ellie tried to go about her work, she couldn't stop thinking about Cameron. Him typing up his sign. Him printing it out. Him getting up early (what colour were his bed sheets – no, not the point). Him coming over in secret to tape up his dumb sign with those big, dumb, strong arms of his…

Had she really gotten under his skin so quickly?

Ellie was about to laugh, but then she realised: if she'd gotten under his skin, he'd gotten under her skin, too…

"Oh, no," Ellie sighed.

For too long, she'd stood at the window and looked at the gym where she knew Cameron worked. Why did it have to be so close to her boutique?

It was well within opening hours for Shoperapy at this point. It would be very unprofessional for Ellie to just close up out of the blue. Why, her first real customer might be moments away from coming in!

But then again, the gym was right there… How long could it really take to just pop over really quickly? For a minute or two? Three tops.

Ellie tapped her manicured nails impatiently against her hip. Deep down, she knew she shouldn't.

But…

Before she could think better of it and change her mind, Ellie wrote a quick 'Be Back Before You Can Say Stiletto' sign, touched up her Chanel red lips (why is not important), locked the door to her boutique, and hurried across the street. A car horn startled her. She'd nearly been hit by oncoming traffic she hadn't even looked for.

It was almost enough to make her turn around. This man was not worth losing a customer over. And this man was certainly not worth dying for.

And yet…

Ellie marched right past reception after swinging the gym door wide open like a righteous storm. Guys did make her a little crazy sometimes – not that she liked Cameron or anything, quite the opposite, actually.

Ellie found Cameron working out with a beautiful woman who looked to be in her 40s. Ellie occasionally did a spin class with Chase, but her workouts never looked like what this woman was doing. Her toned, tight body was covered in sweat, her cheeks bright red, her breathing measured and focused. Had Ellie stumbled into a Nike commercial or something?

She was so distracted that she almost forgot what she came in there for. That was until Cameron started laughing. Laughing... at her!

"So you've ruined my personal life, and now you've come for my professional life?" he demanded, crossing his arms over his broad, muscular chest.

Ellie refused to acknowledge how this made his big biceps stand out quite nicely.

To the woman who was glancing in confusion between her and Cameron while slowly setting down her dumbbell, Ellie said, "Please excuse me. I'm sorry you have to hear this."

This made the woman grin. She looked at Cameron with an amused glint in her eye.

"What did you do?" she asked him.

"Nothing!" Cameron protested. "This lady is crazy."

"This is nothing?" Ellie asked in frustration, waving the crumpled sign, she'd taken back out the trash, at Cameron.

Cameron grinned devilishly. It was horrible. Horrible, because Ellie found it very cute. And distracting. What was she saying? Squinting at the sign, which was balled up anyway, he said, "I don't see my name anywhere on that. How do you know it was me who put it up?"

Ellie laughed. How ridiculous? Was he serious?

"With your contentious personality, miss," Cameron continued, "I wouldn't be surprised if you've gone on the attack with half the men in this town."

Ellie was stunned into silence.

"In fact," Cameron said, wagging a finger. "I think the question should not be who wrote this, but who didn't."

Ellie gritted her teeth.

"I'll have you know that many men find me agreeable and sweet and lovely," she said.

When the woman stuck between them gently reached out for the sign to take a look, Ellie, distracted with glaring at a pair of very nice green eyes, let her. The woman smoothed out the paper and read it as Cameron continued.

"Well then, you're free to go talk to them instead of bothering me," Cameron said before adding with a gesture towards the woman, "And my very important client."

The woman waved her hand dismissively as she read. "Oh, I'm doing just fine," she said. "Don't mind me."

"Believe me," Ellie said, "I would love nothing more than to never see you again in my whole life. You're the one who came poking your stick back at me."

The woman raised an amused eyebrow at Ellie's... interesting... choice of words.

"Metaphorically speaking, of course," Ellie mumbled, cheeks flaring red hot.

"How presumptuous of you," Cameron said with a grin. "You're the last woman in the world I'd poke with my stick. Metaphorical or otherwise."

Ellie narrowed her eyes at Cameron. She was breathing heavily as if it had been her just working out instead of the woman between them.

"How long did it take you to print that out?" she asked. Cameron's jaw tightened.

"No time at all," he said.

"Emhmm," Ellie said, nodding.

"You don't believe me?"

"Not even the tiniest bit," Ellie said.

Why did Ellie have this strange, very strong desire to smile as she argued with this frustrating, arrogant, stubborn man? And why did she get the feeling that he had the exact same strange, very strong desire to smile, too?

"Cameron," the woman said, "what did you do?"

She was holding up the sign to him, a hand on her shapely hip. Cameron didn't look at her. He kept his gaze fixed on Ellie.

"I gave this woman a taste of her own medicine," he said. "This meddlesome, headstrong, pain in the you know what woman."

Ellie was too frustrated to speak a word further to this impossible man. All she could do was make a sound of exacerbation that he seemed to enjoy.

She apologised once more to the woman and was about to leave before she decided to add, "And, really, you don't need a personal trainer anyway, certainly not this one. You look amazing."

Then she went to leave, a quiet storm of annoyance brewing within her. It was only then that she realised it wasn't just Cameron's client who had been listening. It was the whole gym. Every single person had stopped working out to watch her little tete-a-tete with the worst man alive. Embarrassment swallowed her whole as she approached the front desk.

"Um, I, um, I just came in to ask if everything was alright with my membership?" she said to the receptionist, who stared at her with wide eyes.

Ellie was acutely aware of a dozen eyes boring into her back. One pair in particular, she could feel like bony knuckles.

"Let me just check," the receptionist said, glancing away to her computer quickly.

The atmosphere was thick as the seconds ticked away with her clicking on the keys. Ellie's embarrassment tightened its grip around her chest, akin to a corset constricting her breath. Yet, just as the frustration threatened to engulf her entirely, the receptionist's demeanour softened, her features shifting into an expression of genuine empathy.

"Ah, I see the problem here. I truly apologise for this mishap. Let me rectify it," she said, her voice now gentle and sincere, much like a soothing balm on an aching wound.

With a flourish, she handed Ellie a complimentary weekly pass, an unexpected olive branch in the middle of a stormy encounter.

"You're welcome to use this at any time," she said with a wink. Though Ellie took the pass, it felt like receiving a tiny trophy for an unwinnable race. She appreciated the gesture, yet the bubbling annoyance still clung to her like an unwelcome fog. In return, she leaned over and whispered to the receptionist, "I own that shop across the street. 10% off your first purchase for helping a girl out."

The receptionist smiled.

As Ellie turned to exit the reception area, the conflict inside her simmered; her irritation lingered, but the pass gleamed like a distant beacon of possibility. Perhaps it would grant her the chance to truly immerse herself in the groaning machinery of the gym, but she would just need to make sure it was when 'he' was not working.

Ellie resolved to tackle her next visit with a more composed outlook, hopeful that the sour taste of today's encounter with Cameron might be washed away by a large dose of sweat and steadfast determination.

As Ellie walked out of the gym as quickly as she entered, she tried to forget the confrontation. But her mind was filled with conflicting emotions, frustration boiling beneath the surface. The exchange of words echoed mockingly in her ears. Each step she took was deliberate, a conscious effort to forget, and move on.

Walking away was not an admission of defeat but a calculated stride towards personal liberation—she had said her peace. And that was that. But boy, was he cute…

Chapter 7: Victoria Buchanan

Age: 52 (though you'd never know it)

Relationship Status: – Recently divorced after her ex-husband left her for a younger and 'fitter' woman but looking to fall back in love and have a fresh start, which she believes is possible.

Opinion of Love: Believes you can fall in love more than once and doesn't believe in happy ever after as she knows men too well, but is all for happy now.

Style: Elegant, a timeless, and refined approach to fashion and life, characterised by **simplicity, gracefulness, and attention to detail.** Fashion which accentuates your figure and, in Victoria's case, can also cover the areas of your body you don't feel confident to show.

Victoria was halfway out the door of the gym before she realised her arms were bare. She'd been insecure about revealing them ever since her now ex-husband gave her one last tender goodbye on his way out the door of their once happy home: 'Good luck on the market with those batwings, baby.'

Despite how many times she told herself it'd been just plain old cruelty, it had wormed its way under her skin.

She'd moved on from him without all too much trouble, though she did sometimes stalk his Instagram and Twitter accounts. But what was proving to be impossible to move on from was her! Victoria found herself soon no longer looking to see if her ex was happy, but rather if the new woman he was seeing had smaller arms than her. She didn't eat for a whole day after she saw a picture of a woman 17 years her junior… a dancer… and a palates instructor with her tiny arms up in a bright blue sky beside her wolf-grinning ex. That's when she called her nephew, Cameron, for help.

He told her she looked fantastic, and she told him she believed him, but what she really believed was that just a few more months of working out, toning up, and dieting to lose just a little fat would really give her the perfect revenge body.

Then she'd show her ex how she did 'on the market'.

But she wasn't quite there yet, and so after she noticed the cool morning sea breeze on her arms, Victoria hurried back inside the gym with the same kind of panic as if she'd run out in her birthday suit. She snatched up her jacket like it was a towel.

With her arms covered and her confidence back, Victoria dashed back outside, searching the cute street of nice shops and restaurants which led down to the beach for the woman who came in and gave her favourite nephew a piece of her mind. Quite impressively, she might add.

Victoria adored Cameron with all her heart – he'd been her biggest support when she was going through her difficult divorce. He'd helped her get rid of her anger by putting her through kick-boxing workouts at the gym where he worked, going out for long walks with her when she couldn't bear to be in the house alone, and dining in her favourite restaurants when she didn't want to eat alone. Cameron was one of the good guys. But she knew Cameron was just about as stubborn as one could get, and Victoria liked seeing a woman who could give it right back – that was the kind of woman she wanted to be friends with. A warrior. A take-no-bull bull rider. (And it didn't hurt that she dressed impeccably.) She couldn't let that kind of opportunity just run out the door and disappear.

As Victoria scanned the bustling street, her gaze fell upon the woman. In the end, she hadn't been that difficult to find in the crowd: her silhouette, in a gorgeous navy dress, was an alluring contrast to the lively cacophony engulfing them.

Victoria called after her, "Hey! Hey! Wait!"

The woman, her dark hair bustled by the breeze, turned her head slightly, revealing a blend of curiosity and mild concern etched upon her face.

"Is everything alright?" she inquired, her tone reassuring and imbued with warmth.

"Hi, I'm from the gym. I just ran out to say I'm so terribly sorry about my nephew!" Victoria exclaimed, coming to a breathless halt beside her. "Cameron is somewhat of a handful. Sometimes, I have to get away from him, too, for a bit. Thus, why I'm out here talking to you instead of working out!"

A mischievous grin danced across her lips. She wanted to connect with this woman, even if, for a moment, it was at her nephew's expense.

With a gentle chuckle, the woman replied, "He's quite literally the worst man I've had the misfortune to run across. Though, if he's the nephew of a woman like you, I suppose I may have to reconsider."

The woman had a playful grin just like her own, and Victoria instinctively recognised the camaraderie budding between them.

"I'm Victoria, by the way," she said, extending her hand toward what she hoped was a new friend as a sense of excitement bubbled within her.

"Ellie." Victoria smiled.

"Nice to meet you, Ellie. And I must say, you look absolutely fabulous! I often wish I had the confidence to don attire as chic as yours!"

There was admiration in her words, but beneath the surface was a bit of envy Victoria didn't like in herself. Ellie exuded effortless Grace, and she had the arms to wear something Victoria would never.

"Sorry, I shouted at you down the street," Victoria laughed to rid herself of those feelings. "I didn't know what to call you.'

Ellie laughed, "Sure you did. Don't you remember, I'm 'that confrontational, meddling lady' or, as Cameron called me, 'porcupine'?"

Victoria blocked the sun with her hand as she tried to stay out of the way of passing pedestrians with their arms loaded full of shopping bags. It was another side effect of her ex-husband's thoughtlessness: she always felt like she was taking up too much space.

"I really do apologise for my nephew. He's a good guy, really. You must have just gotten off on the completely wrong foot."

Ellie said, "More like the wrong planet."

"Take this how you will," Victoria said, "but it takes something very special to get under Cameron's skin as you've clearly done. Or someone very special."

Victoria thought she sensed a little something between her nephew and Ellie, but this was confirmed when a pink flush as soft as a cherry blossom spread across Ellie's cheek.

So as not to embarrass her, Victoria said, "The truth is I didn't run after you like a crazy lady to talk about my nephew. It's just that I adore your dress."

Ellie beamed as she replied, "It's from a new boutique." "You own a boutique?"

"I sure do!"

"Where is it?" Victoria asked.

In a month or two, maybe three, once she'd really toned up her arms, Victoria thought she would love to buy something similar to what Ellie was wearing. Hopefully, Ellie's boutique wasn't too far...

"It's here," Ellie said.

"Where?" Victoria asked, craning her head around.

Ellie laughed and tapped the window beside it. In elegant lettering, it read: Shoperapy.

"This is your boutique?" Victoria asked, incredulous. "I opened it just last week!"

Victoria cupped her hands to look inside against the glare of the morning sun. It looked beautiful. Like a delicious cupcake, she really shouldn't even have the tiniest taste of it. At least not yet.

"Why don't you come inside?" Ellie asked. "I have this dress in three different colours. Your skin tone would look stunning in the green."

But Victoria shook her head. "Sometime soon, perhaps," she said.

"Nonsense!" Ellie said. "You're right here!"

Victoria felt a wave of panic. She wasn't ready. And she didn't want to admit her silly insecurities to Ellie, even if she did seem beyond sweet. Her mind searched for the easiest excuse: her workout! Yes, she needed to get back to burning calories, tightening muscles, and getting closer to her revenge body.

"I'm sorry," Victoria said, thumbing over her shoulder, "but Cameron's waiting."

Ellie rolled her eyes teasingly.

"Since when is lifting weights more fun than trying on sparkly dresses?"

Victoria shrugged.

"Alright, alright," Ellie said, "but later this week, then." "Umm—I might have a client meeting or—"

"I promise I'll find you something you'll look drop-dead gorgeous in," Ellie pressed. "Maybe for a hubby or boyfriend?"

"Divorced," Victoria said, lifting her empty ring finger. "Even more reason," Ellie said, winking. "Now is the moment

in your life that should be all about discovering what makes you feel empowered—clothes can uplift in ways you never thought possible."

"Can they uplift my arms?" Victoria joked. Ellie seemed stunned.

"Victoria, please don't tell me that man made you feel insecure about your absolutely banging body."

Victoria smiled sheepishly.

"No..." she said slowly. "Of course not..."

Ellie took Victoria's hands and said, "When you enter my boutique later this very week, you will see I have a wealth of designs that can accentuate your figure and boost your self-assurance."

Her eyes were aglow with the prospect of wrangling a new fashionista into her world. Especially one that needed a good dose of self-confidence.

Victoria's heart fluttered. Ellie's generosity was exactly what she'd been missing since her divorce made her see other women as nothing but competition. The warmth encapsulating their conversation enveloped Victoria like a soft embrace, illuminating the apprehensions that had clung to her like shadows. In Ellie's genuine smile, she discerned the flicker of kindness and understanding that seemed almost magical in its ability to dissolve her doubts.

In that instant, as the two women stood together on the busy sidewalk, time itself stilled, allowing an oasis of merriment in the otherwise chaotic ebb and flow of life. They stood encased in their own little bubble of newfound companionship, and Victoria could not be more excited about it.

"So later this week, then?" Ellie pressed. Victoria laughed heartily.

"You may very well have become my new favourite person within a matter of minutes!" she said.

"Thank you," Ellie said. "But I didn't hear a 'yes'."

Victoria shook her head. She understood exactly how her nephew and this woman locked horns. Ellie was just as stubborn as Cameron. Perhaps they were a better match than either of them realised...

"Well?" Ellie said, leaning forward eagerly. "Come on, you'll be turning heads in no time with the right pieces! I've already got my mind set on a few exquisite outfits for you.

"I mean..." Victoria said hesitantly.

"Let's make it happen!" Ellie said, infectious enthusiasm radiating in her tone. "I'll help you discover garments that not only flatter your silhouette but also imbue you with an undaunted sense of confidence!"

She spun with playful flamboyance, conjuring an imaginary wardrobe brimming with possibilities. Victoria could say 'no' no longer.

"Alright!" she cried, throwing her hands up in happy defeat. "You've got me."

"Oh, I've got you alright," Ellie said, pulling Victoria into a big hug.

In that instant, Victoria realised that she had not merely met a stranger in the middle of her workout; she had met a friend in Ellie, while unwittingly stepping into an exhilarating new chapter, overflowing with new adventures that awaited just around the corner.

After Victoria waved goodbye, she realised she'd used up completely the rest of the time for her workout with Cameron. This was surprising to her since she hadn't missed a full workout since the divorce, sacrificing all kinds of things to always be there. And always for the full time.

But what was even more surprising was that she was surprisingly okay with it.

Chapter 8: Jess

As her dinner with Adam quickly approached, Jess began her ritual of getting ready. The scent of her lavender-scented candles lingered in the air, mingling with her excitement. She carefully brushed her long, chestnut hair, allowing it to fall in loose waves around her shoulders. Each stroke of the brush sent a small thrill of anticipation through her; tonight was going to be special. She just knew it.

She applied shimmering eyeshadow to brighten her hazel eyes and make them sparkle like her enthusiasm. Lips painted a soft rose shade completed the look, transforming her in the mirror from the girl who looked and never leapt to someone at long last ready to embrace a new chapter. Standing back to admire her reflection, she couldn't help but smile, a rush of confidence swelling within her.

Until that confidence suddenly dropped as the moment at last arrived: her taxi was pulling up outside.

"What if I'm overdressed?" she thought anxiously.

After all, she wanted to impress Adam without looking like she had tried too hard. Should she go and change? Were the heels too high? Are the lashes too voluminous?

If it hadn't been for the honk of the taxi horn, Jess might not have left her house. But she never liked people to be upset with her, so she hurried out her front door, despite her doubts.

"Just be yourself," she whispered to herself as she click-clacked down her front sidewalk to the curb. "That's what Ellie said, 'Just be yourself,'" she repeated as she climbed inside the back of the taxi.

"What's that, ma'am?" the taxi driver asked.

Jess blushed with embarrassment.

"Nothing," she said. "Sorry."

Except it wasn't nothing. She was so nervous she could hardly remember who she was, let alone how she was supposed to be. Listening to the driver's chit-chat helped Jess take her mind off her twisting stomach, but still, when they pulled up outside the restaurant, her palms were slick on her shaking knees.

The restaurant along the beach looked perfectly charming as Jess walked in, doing her best to just keep putting one foot in front of the other. Dim lights hung from the ceiling, casting a warm glow over the cosy tables. Jess explained to the host that she was here to meet her friend – was that what Adam had called her when he arrived and told the host he was expecting someone? Or had he maybe used another term? Something more than 'friend'.

This is what Jess thought about, chewing at her lip, as the host led her through the restaurant to an outdoor table beneath patio lights strung between leafy trees. Over the ocean was the most brilliant sunset.

Immediately upon seeing her, Adam stood up so abruptly that he nearly knocked over his chair. Jess tried not to laugh, but she found it immensely charming.

"Here you are," Adam said, smoothing down his tie as his eyes shone on her as brightly as the sunset on the water.

Jess smiled.

"Here I am!" she said shyly.

Adam then did something that he'd never done before as 'just friends': he took her hand in his and spun her around to admire her outfit. It made Jess feel amazing. Adam gave her his full attention, his eyes shimmering with genuine interest.

At that moment, it felt as if he had cast a spell on her, allowing her to feel as if she was the only person in the packed restaurant. Just being so close to Adam was a reminder of the extraordinary potential of the evening. It made Jess weak in the knees, so she was more than thankful when Adam pulled out her chair for her and helped her to get seated.

Jess was so pleased she was wearing her outfit from Shoperapy, feeling more beautiful than she had in years. Ellie had been right: the pink midi dress she'd bought was perfect for a summer date (it was a date, right?), with its light chiffon material and floaty skirt making her feel feminine. Her matching shimmering gold sandals added just that little bit of needed sparkle to her outfit. As Adam poured her a glass of chilled rose, Jess made a quick note to thank Ellie and write a glowing review for her on Instagram. "Cheers," Adam said, lifting his glass (filled with water since he was driving).

Jess raised her glass to meet his, but hesitated. "What are we toasting to?" she asked.

Adam thought for a moment, and while what he came up with was only a single word, Jess knew there was nothing else she would have wanted to hear.

"Us!" Adam answered cheerfully.

"To us," Jess said, tapping her glass against his. It made the sound of pure magic.

She was there. She could feel the chair beneath her, could feel the salt air on her cheek, could feel Adam's eyes on her downturned gaze, and yet Jess still couldn't quite believe she was out to dinner with the man she'd had a crush on since the second she saw him all those years ago at new employee orientation. She almost laughed thinking of those horrible old videos about office policies and appropriate conduct.

The conversation flowed easily. It shouldn't have been a surprise: they'd known each other for so long and had become almost instant friends. But Jess was happy nonetheless – it was going well.

Jess glanced over her menu at Adam, who happened to glance up at her over his menu at the exact same moment. She smiled, and her cheeks grew warm. It was a wonderful feeling.

The two friends looked over the menu. Jess scanned the options with a hint of anticipation. She was particularly drawn to the feta cheese salad, its vibrant colours, and the thought of tangy cheese tantalising her taste buds.

"I think I might go for the salad," she murmured, her eyes gleaming with excitement.

Jess loved fresh flavours, and the idea of a light, healthy meal made her feel invigorated.

Adam tapped his finger thoughtfully on the menu. A moment later, he set the menu down contentedly.

"I reckon I'll have the steak pie; it sounds delicious!" he declared. "Hey, do you remember that first lunch we went to as trainees that first week? I'm pretty sure that's what I ordered then, too."

Jess was over the moon. Not with his choice of dinner, though a steak pie did sound delicious. But with the fact that he'd been thinking of exactly what she'd been thinking of.

As they placed their orders with the waitress, a sense of excitement enveloped the table. Jess smiled at Adam. They were not just ordering a meal – they were creating memories, filled with laughter and the simple joy of enjoying good food together. Without the menus to look at, it was just them. Eye to eye. Jess felt a little nervous as they both laughed and awkwardly sipped their drinks.

Soon, their food arrived, and Jess was barely able to concentrate on her plate, far too enamoured she was with Adam's presence. Then again, she noticed that he didn't seem to be eating much of his plate either. Could it be that he was enamoured, too?

As the night went on, they shared jokes and laughs that echoed around the restaurant, a stark contrast to the fluttering butterflies in Jess's stomach. They shared stories about their childhood, their hilarious school incidents, and their dreams for the future. Every now and then, their eyes would meet, and Jess felt her heart skip a beat.

Jess couldn't stop touching her cheeks. She knew she was ruining her makeup, but they felt so warm, and the muscles were practically sore from smiling so much. She was sure her cheeks were bright pink and that Adam had surely noticed. But there was really nothing she could do about it – she was happy, pure, and simply happy. Happier than she could remember being in a long time.

Just as they finished their meal, Jess realised she had dribbled sauce at the corner of her mouth. Mortified, she grabbed a napkin to dab it away, but in her panic, she knocked over her glass of rose.

It splattered across the table and, to her utter horror, splashed onto Adam's shirt!

"Oh no! I'm so sorry!" Jess gasped, while Adam erupted into laughter, wiping at his shirt with a napkin.

"Honestly, Jess, you've really made this meal unforgettable! It'll just add character to my shirt," he joked, his eyes twinkling. Jess couldn't help but laugh, too, relieved that Adam wasn't put off by the mishap.

As they headed outside, Jess felt lighter, sure that there was an open pathway ahead of her.

"So, shall we do this again?" Adam asked. "This?" Jess asked.

She knew the word she wanted to hear: date.

But Adam jostled her playfully with his elbow and said, "Yeah, 'this', ruining my clothes."

It was obviously a joke, and Jess laughed, but she was left feeling uncertain. Did Adam mean another date? Or another dinner between friends? How was she supposed to know?

Adam suggested a walk along the beach. That was romance, wasn't it? Jess thought. That definitely signalled date, didn't it?

The cool breeze swept their faces as Jess stole glances at Adam to try and read his expression. That had been more than a casual dinner, hadn't it? It had to have been. Yes, by the end of their walk, Jess was sure it had been a date, sure that the next one, too, would be a date, sure this was the start of something real at last.

Adam offered to drive Jess home. As he drove her home, Jess was giddy with excitement, but also trepidation. Her relationship with

Adam was one of, if not the most important, relationships in her life. Was she risking too much, wanting more?

But then she remembered the twirl at the restaurant and the touch of his fingers on hers, and she was sure once more that there was something more there... wasn't there?

The whole way to her house, Jess went back and forth, back and forth in her mind. What was going to happen? Would he try and kiss her? What would she do if he did? Was she ready for that? Of course, she was! Wasn't she?

Adam pulled up to the curb outside her house. This was the moment. This was it.

Jess's eyes fluttered closed as Adam leaned towards her. Goodbye, friend zone. Hello, true love.

Jess's lips parted, eager for the touch of his kiss and...

J: No kiss.

E: Oh, no!

J: I really thought there'd be a kiss...

E: What about a lean-in?

E: Tell me there was at least a lean-in for a kiss.

J: There was a lean, alright...

E: See, that's something!

J: He leaned over to grab my to-go box from the floor of the car.

E: Oh, my.

J: I know.

J: I'm giving up.

E: You are doing no such thing.

E: Don't worry.

E: We just need more sparkle.

Chapter 9: Ellie

Ellie had tidied the stack of colourful cashmere sweaters with cute bow details five times already – but what else was there to do? There wasn't a customer in sight. Despite all her efforts, Shoperapy was still like the shy wallflower at the prom. She was just waiting for someone to approach and ask her to dance. Oh, how her boutique wanted to dance! With energy, with enthusiasm, with joy. If only she'd be given the chance...

Running her fingers across soft cashmere, Ellie admired the way it shimmered subtly in the light, as if it held the promise of warmth and comfort. She was sure it would change some woman's life one day. It would give her just that little extra bit of confidence or cause her next love to glance back just that one extra time, and it would make all the difference. But none of that would ever happen if no one ever came in to try the sweater on...

After watching pedestrians pass right by her shop without hardly turning their heads, Ellie decided to sort through the delicate fabrics draped across the mannequin display in the window. Perhaps that would entice customers in. Sunlight filtered in through the large window, yet Ellie felt the weight of the empty shop pressing down on her spirit. The stunning colours and textures brought little joy to her at that moment; they merely reminded her of the silence.

Despite her best efforts to attract customers with thoughtfully arranged displays and enticing clothes, the shop remained quiet. Her heart sank at the thought of yet another day without a sale. She looked through the window, watching again as passers-by walked along briskly, their laughter and chatter echoing through the streets. They lingered at café menus and famous high-end shoe brands, yet they never lingered at her shop.

"Perhaps they're not in the mood for sparkle today," she mused, forcing a faint smile.

But deep down, she felt a pang of disappointment, a nagging feeling that perhaps her shop wasn't good enough or that they didn't see the beauty she so cherished.

Hope flickered dimly within her as she considered that maybe soon, someone would discover her little haven—her quiet fashion shop, waiting patiently for a customer to ignite its spark.

People crossed back and forth outside the shop, but still, no one came inside. Why? Why? Ellie just didn't understand!

She'd worked tirelessly to promote her fashion boutique, pouring her heart and soul into every effort. Each day, she meticulously updated her social media presence, posting vibrant photos on Facebook and Instagram that showcased her latest collections. Her careful attention to detail ensured that every post was not only visually appealing but also resonated with her audience. Well, the audience she one day hoped to have.

In addition to her online updates, Ellie printed an eye-catching array of flyers that she strategically placed around town. Community boards, coffee shop doors, and even the benches along the beach. Bold, artistic fonts adorned the glossy paper – they were the very definition of eye-catching! She announced special promotions left and right. She pulled out every trick in the bag to build up intrigue. She made her words sound like a personal invite to potential customers.

She believed that her creativity in her promotional efforts would help her stand out in a competitive industry, but, her efforts weren't paying off.

What was missing?

She never thought it would be this hard, to start a business. And if she didn't turn things around quickly, Shoperapy wouldn't make it to its first month anniversary, let alone through its first year.

Ellie's head was hidden in her arms, collapsed over the cash register in despair, when the soft chime of the bell above the door. She barely registered it – she'd become so used to the silence.

"Um... hello?"

Ellie's head popped up. A customer! Could it be? Could this be the single snowflake that triggers the avalanche?

But it was a familiar face hesitating in the doorway. "Victoria!" Ellie said, coming out from behind the desk. "Is this a bad time?" Victoria asked.

"No, no," Ellie insisted, shaking her head. "Sorry, I thought you were a customer."

Victoria laughed.

"But I am a customer," she said, holding up her purse as if proof.

Ellie hugged her new friend in greeting.

"I don't see you as a customer," she said.

Victoria clicked her tongue.

"Ellie, if you make every woman who walks through that door your friend, who will be left to be customers?" she asked.

Ellie hesitated. Did Victoria have a point?

"I run my own business, my freelance business," Victoria said. "I know how tough it can be. You have to be ruthless."

Ellie could use many words to describe herself, but 'ruthless' would not be one. Well, one time, she said Chale's white loafers made him look like a retiree...

"Is it really so impossible to help women and make some money?" Ellie asked with a note of hopelessness in her voice.

Victoria winked and replied, "How about we see?" Ellie grew excited.

"So, you're here to shop?" she asked.

Victoria sighed and explained, "Why not? I was sitting at home and scrolling through Instagram when I saw a picture of my ex and her sunning themselves in Milan, and it just set me off, so it was either a glass of wine or dress shopping. I would have picked a glass of wine, but I did make that promise to come let you try and do your magic."

Ellie tapped her nose and said, "Hold on."

She emerged from the back room with a bottle of wine and two glasses.

"Two birds, one stone," she laughed.

The two women raised a toast to Milan falling into a giant sinkhole, and then Ellie showed Victoria to the dressing rooms.

"Wow, Ellie!" Victoria exclaimed.

They were charmingly vintage, the two little rooms. It was like stepping back in time to an era of elegance and softness. The air was tinged with a subtle blend of musk and lavender— a fragrance that lingered from the beautifully handcrafted garments hanging on wooden hangers, their fabric rich with intricate details.

A large antique mirror, framed in aged gold, rested against the wall outside the dressing rooms. Beside it, a hat stand showcased a collection of feathered fascinators and wide-brimmed hats. Victoria touched one with a suede fringe.

"You can't forget accessories," Ellie said.

"Certainly not," Victoria agreed. "Just like a prenup."

They both laughed. Then, Ellie, had Victoria get comfy and run off to start picking some selections. Spirits had been high, but as the light pink suede curtain rustled and rustled, but never opened, Ellie could feel the storm cloud shifting overhead. There was really no denying this when a sundress came flying from over the top of the dressing room and landed on Ellie's head.

"No need to panic," Ellie said, re-emerging from beneath all that fabric. "That was only the first!"

"I tried on six before that," Victoria said with a moan. "You didn't let me see them," Ellie cried.

"Oh, believe me, you didn't want to see this car crash." "Car crash?" Ellie echoed.

Victoria poked her head out from the curtain, her normally perfectly styled grey-streaked hair messy as a little owl.

"Oh, Ellie, it's not your dresses," she said. "The dresses are all stunning, fabulous, amazing. It's me.'

Ellie was truly flabbergasted – Victoria had an incredible figure! But beyond that, Ellie's goal was to make women of all shapes and sizes look and feel good. She knew someone didn't have to fit into the traditional standards of beauty to look great. But then again, Victoria was as 'ideal' as it got.

This was proving to be a more difficult case than Ellie first suspected. She understood that there was more to making a woman feel good than just putting them in a dress that objectively looked good. She tapped her chin, thinking, as Victoria disappeared back inside the curtain.

"If you'd just let me see you in one of the dresses…" Ellie tried.

From inside the room, Victoria called, "No, no. I still have a few more here to try. It's alright."

Ellie was stumped. This was going to take all her focus. All her attention. It might be tireless hours. But she was going to give Victoria her entire focus and make sure she left Shoperapy feeling amazing.

But, of course, that was the very moment that the shop door swung open. Was it a case of being careful what you asked for? Ellie had, after all, wanted a boutique full of customers. And now that she couldn't handle them, here they were. Except it wasn't a customer, after all. It was another friend.

It was Grace.

Ellie watched as Grace, in her ice cream shop outfit, collapsed dramatically on the big, comfy velvet couch in the centre of her boutique. She looked entirely distraught, with bright red cheeks and ice cream on her nose.

"I don't know what to do!" Grace cried, throwing her arms over her face.

Oh, no, two emergencies at once. Ellie never was a great multitasker.

"Victoria, dear, do you mind giving me a moment?"

Victoria's reply was only to throw another failed dress over the top of the dressing room. Ellie was wondering if the calm of the morning hadn't been so bad after all as she hurried over to Grace.

"Talk to me," Ellie said, sitting beside the girl.

"Oh, Ellie, it's horrible," Grace moaned. "Everett – that's his name, by the way. He finally gained the courage to introduce himself the fifth time he came in – Everett kept coming in and making me smile. And he keeps asking me thoughtful questions about myself. And, what's worse, I'm really starting to look forward to him coming in each day for ice cream."

Ellie laughed. Wasn't that funny: Victoria was upset with her perfect hourglass figure, and Grace was upset with a charming guy who seemed totally into her. And her? Well, maybe Ellie didn't need to be so upset about Shoperapy's slow start. After all, she was living her dream.

Slumping even further into the couch, Grace said, "He gets so distracted talking with me at the cash register that half his ice cream cone drips over his hand."

Well, didn't that just sound horrible? "And?" Ellie asked.

"And he's nice and sweet and cute," Grace said.

"And?" Ellie asked again, really not seeing the big problem Grace seemed to see.

"And he treats me kindly, and yesterday he told me my smile

makes his day."

"And?"

Finally, Grace flung her arms up into the air, "And what if Tim comes back?"

Ellie understood now why Grace was so distraught when she should have been excited about a nice guy who liked her. Ellie was trying to think of the best way to word her advice when Victoria came out of the dressing room. Ellie did a double take. Wait, could it be?

It was!

Victoria was in one of Ellie's dresses!

And, of course, she looked absolutely dynamite. But she wasn't looking even the slightest towards the mirror; she stood not a meter from it. Ellie wanted to grab her new friend by the shoulders, steer her around, and cry, 'Can't you see how amazing you look?!'

But Victoria had such an impassioned look on her face, that Ellie remained seated and silent.

"Excuse me," Victoria said to Grace, "I was changing just now, and I happened to overhear what you were saying, and I just had to come out and say something."

Grace looked up in awe at Victoria.

"Umm… yeah, sure," she said with a hint of confusion in her voice.

Victoria sat on the armrest of the couch and took Grace's hands into her own. Grace glanced at Ellie for an explanation, but Ellie hardly knew what was going on either.

In a tone both firm, but tender, Victoria said, "It's taken me a long time in life to learn this, but it's the truest thing you'll ever hear: A man will show you if he's interested just like he will show you if he's not. It's not complicated."

Grace tried to protest.

"But—"

"Everett likes you," Victoria said. And then, "Tim does not."

After such a bold declaration, there was utter silence in the boutique. Outside came the murmur of shoppers on their way. But inside, it was as if everyone was holding their breath. Ellie was worried that Grace might have found Victoria too blunt, too harsh. She certainly hadn't held anything back. There was no sugar coating to her advice. It wasn't exactly how Ellie would have delivered the news...

And yet, a moment later, Grace smiled. It was a weak smile, a rather sad smile, but a smile nonetheless.

Sighing, Grace said, "You're right. I wish you weren't. But you're right. Thank you."

Victoria squeezed Grace's hands.

"I wish I weren't right, too, my dear," she said.

Both women smiled.

Victoria laughed, "Look at me, storming out in a dress I clearly can't pull off. I better go change."

"Are you serious?" Grace replied. "That dress is stunning on you.

I wish I had your figure, all those womanly curves. An hourglass has nothing on you!"

Victoria tried to say no, that it didn't work on her at all. But Grace suddenly hopped up from the couch and took Victoria to the mirror.

"Just look, would you," Grace said.

Victoria avoided her reflection till Grace stomped her foot in determination. Ellie laughed. She'd never seen Grace so imposing. She was normally so shy, so timid. But she was going to force Victoria to admit how good she looked whether she wanted to or not. Good for her, Ellie thought.

Ellie watched as Victoria slowly, but surely met her reflection in the mirror. The dress was a deep emerald green. Its lustrous fabric shimmered under the soft light. The bodice was intricately embellished with delicate lace. Even though Ellie and Grace were both grinning from ear to ear, sure that this was the dress, Victoria's brow was still furrowed in disappointment.

"Hold on," Grace said.

She dashed off and returned with a low-brim sun hat. Ellie was about to speak up, but that didn't go at all. But Grace moved with such confidence. She knew what she was doing. So, Ellie let her do it.

Placing the hat on Victoria's head, Grace adjusted the brim so it covered her face, but still let her see from the neck down in the mirror.

"Now, imagine you see this woman on the street," Grace said. Ellie smiled. Grace's enthusiasm was infectious. As she spoke, telling Victoria what she saw, she painted a picture of glamour that contrasted sharply with Victoria's unease. The green dress, in Grace's eyes, transformed Victoria into a vision of elegance, someone who was ready to waltz into a grand ballroom. "Well, what do you think now?" Grace asked at last.

Victoria hesitated a moment. Ellie wasn't sure Grace's magic had worked. Slowly, Victoria removed her hat. Grace watched her face eagerly for any sign of what she was thinking.

"How about this," Victoria said, breaking into a grin, "how about if you give Everett a try, I'll give this dress a try?"

It was Grace's turn to bite her lip, unsure. Ellie wanted to shout: Come on, Grace! Say yes! It was so difficult to stay silent and still on the couch...

Grace suddenly stuck out a small hand. Victoria smiled and shook it.

"Deal?" she asked.

"Deal," Grace said.

Ellie, at last, took that as her cue to jump up.

With an enthusiastic clap, she said, "Shall I wrap it up for you then?"

Victoria gave her a playful grin.

"You know, Ellie," she said, "you've got something very special here. Women supporting women is something I'll always support."

Ellie couldn't agree more. She hadn't planned for the morning to go like this. Her whole mind had been filled with dollar signs and overdue bills and rent payments. But this, this was what it should be all about.

How had she so easily forgotten?

She promised herself as Grace and Victoria chatted, quickly getting to know one another, that she would hold onto this beating heart of Shoperapy in the future. In fact, it had given her a rather brilliant idea…

Instagram:

@ellie-vator

Calling All Women: The Heartbroken, The Heartless, and The Heart Filled

Join a supportive, welcoming, stylish community for a night of womanhood, clothes, and complimentary bubbles!

Get to know the women of your town you pass on the street every day. We can do more than admire each other's handbags, ladies!

Starting at 8 pm. Don't worry about what to wear – we've got you covered. Shoperapy @ the corner of Skyler Street.

Chapter 10: Victoria

Victoria was dying. Today's workout session at the gym was the hardest she'd ever had by far. Cameron looked the same (with his usual fitted T-shirt and gym shorts); he didn't seem the same. As Victoria hoisted the dumbbells over her head for what felt like the millionth time, her nephew appeared to be a world away. He was normally a very enthusiastic motivator, but so far, he'd hardly said a word. He wasn't even counting down her reps like usual.

In fact, Victoria had little idea how many she'd done. Or, more importantly, how many she had left to do. She just kept lifting as Cameron paced back and forth, glancing at the clock every few minutes, an unconscious habit he'd had since he was young. She knew exactly what it meant: something was distracting him.

But it was more than just a run-of-the-mill distraction. Of this, she was certain (that, and that her arms were burning!)

Victoria could feel the tension radiating from him. Earlier, he'd called out commands with a slightly sharper tone than usual. 'Come on, push harder! You can do it!' he'd barked.

Instead of the usual high-fives, there had been only a brief nod of acknowledgement. And now? Only sulky silence.

Victoria thought that Cameron had said she would do 12 reps, but she was pretty sure she hit 12 a long time ago. Her arms felt like she'd hit 120 a long time ago.

"Cameron?" Victoria asked.

Nothing.

"Cameron?"

Nothing.

Victoria knew she needed to get to the bottom of what was bothering him. And, more urgently, she needed to get rid of these weights. Why not kill two birds with one stone?

"Ow!" she cried out after suddenly dropping her weights.

The dumbbells hadn't touched her, but Cameron didn't need to know that. At least not yet.

Grabbing at her toe, Victoria hobbled to the bench as Cameron, having been snapped out of his faraway trance, hurried over with panic in his eyes.

"Oh, my gosh, Aunt Vic," he cried, kneeling in front of her to look at her foot, "I am so sorry!"

"Ah, so now you see me," Victoria said, "now that my toe is absolutely crushed beyond repair."

She did her best to hold back her smile as Cameron clutched at the sides of his hair.

"Is it bad?" he asked fearfully. "Oh, Aunt Vic. I swear I was only distracted for a second!"

Victoria rocked back and forth on the bench, squeezing her completely unharmed toe.

"What could have possibly distracted you from your favourite Aunt in the whole wide world?"

This was the most important part of her plan: getting the truth out of the stubborn bugger. From previous experience with her nephew, she knew it was sometimes a difficult feat. If he didn't want to fess up, it was like pulling teeth, getting answers. This time was no different as Cameron hesitated and said, "Oh, it's nothing."

Victoria leaned in closer. Put on her Serious Auntie Eyes.

"Cameron…"

Her nephew sat back on his heels with a huff.

"Really, Aunt Vic. It's nothing."

Victoria sighed. The game continued. She'd maybe lost the battle, but she wouldn't lose the war.

"Treadmill next?" she asked, hopping up.

Cameron glanced after her in surprise.

"What about your toe?"

Victoria shrugged.

"It's nothing, really," she said, repeating his own words back at him.

Cameron's eyes narrowed momentarily in a flash of suspicion, but he still followed after her towards the cardio machines in the gym.

As Victoria suspected, it happened again on the treadmill.

Cameron was supposed to tell her when to stop (he was her personal trainer, after all). But the half-mile she was supposed to run came and went, and he hadn't even glanced at her treadmill's display. He kept looking towards the front of the gym… Victoria's mind was quickly working just as hard as her legs.

What was it about the front of the gym? Why did he keep looking there? There was nothing there. It was just where people entered and left, there and gone…

Victoria almost tripped over her feet when it hit her. The front of the gym was the exact spot where, just a week or so ago, Ellie came storming in like a mad thunderstorm.

Though she was huffing and puffing and sweaty on the treadmill, Victoria smiled, because she was pretty sure now she knew exactly what was distracting her young nephew.

She tried a couple of times to get his attention. She wiped her brow exaggeratedly with her (thankfully) soft face cloth. She guzzled water from her new Stanley Cup, a present from her normally very sweet, very attentive nephew. He didn't notice that she was giving her best performance since she was a tree in her elementary school play.

Finally, Victoria decided to take drastic action: she pretended to faint, tumbling dramatically (but safely) off the treadmill. She even yelled loudly, "Ahh!"

Cameron was horrified as he turned off the machine and rushed to her side. Victoria viewed all of this through thinly peeked eyes.

"You're not dead, are you?" Cameron asked.

"No, but nearly," Victoria cried with an arm flung over her forehead.

Cameron fanned her with a gym brochure and offered her water from the water cooler. He helped her to sit up. His face was red with sheepish embarrassment.

"You just about killed your aunt, Cameron," Victoria said. "How do you feel about that?"

Cameron was super apologetic. He promised it'd never happen again. Yes, Victoria had him right where she wanted him. It was time to spring her trap.

Carefully, Victoria said, "It must have been something... very important you were thinking about..."

Cameron shook his head immediately. Victoria bristled inside.

He was yet again trying to downplay his distraction.

"Maybe I throw in a free massage from the gym physio for your troubles?" he said.

And now he was trying to change the subject. Victoria would not be fooled so easily. She steered the conversation right back where she wanted it.

"A girl, perhaps?" Victoria teased.

Cameron threw his arms up in frustration. He must have known she was onto him.

"It's nothing, Aunt Vic!"

"You must really like her to have made your poor Aunt suffer!" she said, struggling to hold back a grin.

Cameron crossed his arms stubbornly.

"There is no 'her'."

Victoria stared Cameron down, and finally, he rolled his eyes and huffed like he was a teenager again.

"She's horrible."

Victoria laughed: she knew it! Cameron liked Ellie!

"Look," Cameron said, "I want nothing more than to get her out of his mind, but she just won't leave."

He was gritting his teeth. He was clearly upset. But this was all making Victoria very happy.

Most likely just to escape the conversation, Cameron went to get Victoria an ice pack. She suspected they both knew she wasn't injured. As she iced her knee, she decided she wasn't yet done with him.

"You know," she said gently, "I quite like her."

After a moment, she added with a wink for her nephew's sake, "Not that I have any idea who you're talking about."

Victoria hugged her nephew and headed out of the gym, feeling like she'd accomplished something. No, it wasn't a personal best with the weights.

How best should she help stubborn-headed Cameron and Ellie? Was it too far to set up an 'accidental' meeting? Her mind went into overdrive as she considered how to do this, but she knew in the end that Cameron would never allow it.

She had a half hour to spare and decided to take a stroll in the park. She reminisced about how difficult it had been for Cameron to date again after his last relationship ended. It had been a shock to everyone who knew them as a couple.

They'd been quintessential childhood sweethearts. They finished each other's sentences. They were, until the end, that is, inseparable. Everyone in their small town had anticipated a marriage, a family, even someday. But Victoria knew better than most that life had a way of throwing unexpected curves.

Victoria vividly recalled the look in Cameron's eyes when he shared with her his breakup. The mixture of confusion and hurt that crossed his face was a sight that would haunt her for days. In an instant, everything Cameron had built with Laura had come crashing down.

His jokes during that time sounded a lot like the ones she'd heard from Ellie that he was swearing off women. That he was done with love. That he was better off without the heartbreak, which he now saw as inevitable.

They were two little broken peas in a pod, Ellie and Cameron. Victoria couldn't help but smile at the idea of it. Bristling at each other from past hurt. Ignoring what was right in front of them. Flawed in the exact same way.

She hoped they put their stubbornness aside long enough to give themselves a chance.

Victoria continued to sit on the park bench for another ten minutes, people watching, wondering what their stories were, their heartbreak or joy. The crisp air filled her lungs, revitalising her spirit. It was nice to know that love was still in the air, even if it was being swatted away like a fly. It made her feel like she still had a chance, too.

As she started to walk home, she bumped into Sophie, the receptionist from the gym.

"Victoria, are you alright?" Sophie asked. "I heard you fell off the treadmill."

Victoria laughed.

"The only thing that is hurt is my ego," she said.

Sophie was glad to hear it. Then, something clearly popped into her head.

"Hey, do you know what was up with Cameron today?" she asked. "He got his first complaint from a customer. They said it was like he wasn't even there. That's so not like him, right?"

Victoria leaned in conspiratorially.

"You didn't hear it from me, but I think Cameron has been struck by the love bug."

Sophie's eyes went wide with intrigue. She leaned in even closer.

"It's not that cute lady from the other day, is it?" she asked in a whisper. "The one that owns the new boutique on the corner? She gave me a 10% discount, you know."

Victoria grinned.

"Ellie," she said. "And my lips are sealed."

Sophie covered her mouth with excitement.

"She gave him a right mouthful the other day," she said.

"That she did," Victoria agreed, feeling proud of her new friend.

"If you ask me," Sophie said, thinking through, "the two of them are a match made in heaven. That's the best fun I've had in a while at work, watching the two of them arguing." Victoria replied, winking, "Oh, watch this space…"

She knew she certainly would be. Two broken hearts who've each given up on love? It sounded exactly like a recipe for forever to her.

Chapter 11: Jess

Jess sat in her cubicle, wearing her favourite skirt and blouse. She even wore her killer heels to give her an air of confidence. She was feeling far from confident, but faked it till you made it and all that. The bright floral pattern of her blouse usually lifted her spirits, but today, the colours seemed to dim in the shadow of her thoughts. It had been hours since her 'non-date' with Adam, and she cringed when she thought about that moment: her lips pursed... eyes closing, closing, closing... awaiting what she had imagined would be a perfect kiss...

The memory replayed in her mind like an unwelcome film, the moment stretching on as she leaned in, only to find Adam reaching for her to-go box from the restaurant. It had been on the floor matt of the passenger side. When she realised her terrible mistake, she hastily threw on a smile that felt like a mask. 'Goodnight then!' she'd shouted before darting out of the car and running up her drive.

Thinking about it all made her cheeks flush pink all over again. Glancing at the clock on her desk, Jess realised that the hands had barely moved since the last time she'd looked. The stillness of time was maddening, no doubt about that.

Just then, Adam's laughter erupted across the office, light and buoyant, cutting through her reverie. Curiosity got the better of her, and Jess peered over the partition of her cubicle. Her heart skipped a beat when she caught sight of him. He was surrounded by a group of colleagues who seemed unable to contain their mirth. There he was, just as he'd always been. Was it only her that hadn't slept a wink since that night?

Jess leaned in closer, hoping to spy just one single thing about him that seemed to have changed. Just any tiny ray of hope that things were different now. Or it could be... But the way he held his coffee cup was steady and relaxed. The sound of his laughter flowed freely, resonating through the air like music. No sign of tension, restless thoughts or sleepless nights.

Half hidden behind her cubicle, Jess even went as far as to study the colour of his tie. It was a deep navy, a colour she'd always told him she liked. Was that a sign? Had he worn that tie for her? Or was it just a tie to him? Jess worried she might be going insane. This wasn't normal behaviour, was it?

Not that it stopped her, of course.

The way he checked his wristwatch, tilting his head slightly, sparked a memory of their recent conversations. They had talked about time, how it seemed to slip away when they were enjoying themselves. But it was nothing more than that, in the end: a busy civil engineer making sure he wasn't late for his next meeting.

He was just Adam—the organisational wizard of their office, the witty guy who cracked jokes even in the most serious of meetings.

Jess was just about to sink back into her chair of dejection when suddenly, Adam glanced in her direction, catching her eye. The moment felt electric, the air thick with unspoken words. A smile flickered across his lips, and she felt her heart race. Was there an unspoken understanding? Did he know what had almost happened? Was he agonising over that moment, too? Or was it just her imagination playing tricks again?

Despite her attempts to appear unfazed, the blush creeping into her cheeks betrayed her. Jess quickly ducked back down behind her cubicle wall, her mind racing. She couldn't do this. It was too much of a strain on her heart. And she wasn't getting any work done. She couldn't be heartbroken and unemployed.

There was only one solution: avoid Adam.

A difficult task, given that he was a coworker in the same office. Difficult, given they had meetings all throughout the day together. Difficult, given that all she wanted to do was look at his face all day.

But what had to be done had to be done.

Jess heard the conversation just across from her wrapping up and knew that Adam would be making his way towards her any second. That wouldn't do. Keeping her head low beneath the line of cubicles, Jess snuck off with her laptop tucked under her arm. The machine had a terrific battery life – she could avoid returning to her desk to recharge for hours.

It went exceedingly well, Jess's day of hide-and-seek. Yes, she felt a bit childish at times. Nothing says high school quite like eating your lunch in the bathroom with your feet up on the seat instead of down at the canteen. And, yes, it was a little embarrassing to walk into meetings ten minutes late and ask a colleague to scoot over instead of taking the seat Adam saved for her. But it meant she got a lot of extra steps in that day. Less heartache, stronger heart.

Win, win!

Finally, there was only one meeting left. One last hurdle to leap before she was home free.

In the conference room, desks were arranged in a circle, and papers were distributed. Jess sat down between two colleagues. The only other desk was far to the side. She was sure Adam wouldn't ask anyone to move to sit next to her. He was too polite. But then he did just that.

"Busy day?" Adam asked, leaning in far too close.

Jess couldn't look at him. She couldn't even really open her mouth to answer. All she could do was nod quickly and keep her eyes fixed on the presentation screen.

It was the greatest relief when her boss entered the conference room and jumped right into things. But as the meeting went on, Adam would pass her papers or ask for a pen, any excuse to talk to her or move in towards her. Each time it happened, Jess could feel her heart race with a mix of hope and apprehension. What if he decided it was time to clear the air? She couldn't allow herself to think that way. Instead, she buried herself in her notes, tapping her pen nervously against the desk.

As the presentation continued, Jess tried to concentrate on her boss, but her mind kept drifting to the man beside her. Adam's arm brushed against hers as he adjusted his chair. Jess's breath caught in her throat when he asked softly, "Hey, can we talk about the other night?"

The room was dim, the lights low, and the intensity of his gaze when she dared a quick look sent a jolt of fear through her. Panic enveloped her. She could smell his aftershave, a mixture of cedarwood and musk that sent her heart fluttering despite the growing dread.

The term 'the other night' felt like the fuse leading to an explosive conversation she desperately wanted to avoid. Jess feared that if he were to utter those words, what she held in her heart would come crashing down. It was a thought she couldn't bear to contemplate. She drew her hand closer to her lap, trying to suppress the torrent of emotions rising within her.

Her mind raced with worst-case scenarios. What if he was about to tell her that he saw her solely as a friend, that the chemistry they'd shared was something more platonic? The word 'friend' cut deep; it would be the end of the wonderful daydream she had cherished for so long. She realised she had loved Adam from the moment she first laid eyes on him, in the very same conference room where they now sat. It all meant too much for it to end like this.

"I'm sorry," Jess said, "I think my phone is ringing."

It was the lamest excuse. And it wasn't true. But she had to get out of there.

"Jess—"

Adam reached for her, but she stood up abruptly to leave. Too abruptly. She saw the jolted table rock her coworker's coffee cup. She saw it wobbling, almost righting itself. She saw her hand reaching to catch it and only making it worse.

The entire room went silent as the coffee spilt over all the documents and half her coworkers' laps. Jess felt a rush of shame wash over her, cheeks flushing as she fumbled to try to clean up the mess. But it was no use.

"I... I'm sorry," she stammered before running out without even taking her things.

It was perhaps the most embarrassing thing to happen to her at work, but somewhere in her heart, Jess entertained a flicker of relief. The laughter and curious glances of her colleagues were one thing. But hearing Adam's inevitable declaration was quite another. She'd traded the bad for the worst.

As Jess hurried to the bathroom, where she would hide till everyone had left for the day, she was glad she hadn't heard it. That dreadful final nail in the coffin: "Jess, we're friends."

That would have shattered her heart. Instead, all that remained broken was her ego. It felt like a small price to pay for preserving the fragile hope she clung to despite it all. Perhaps soon, she would find the courage to face Adam, but for now, avoidance was the only way she knew how.

So it was back to the bathroom. Back to putting her feet up on the toilet seat. Back to hiding like she was sixteen again. Except this time, the school bully was her heart.

Jess only wished one thing: that she'd brought a snack…

Jess to Ellie: I'm supposed to be in a meeting.

E to J: Well, where are you?

J to E: In a maintenance closet…

J to E: Hiding from Adam…

J to E: Like I did yesterday.

J to E: And the day before yesterday.

J to E: And, well, you get the picture.

E to x: Oh, Jess.

E to J: You poor thing.

J to E: What if he doesn't feel towards me what I feel towards him?

J to **E**: I just can't bear it anymore.

E to **J**: I know what you need.

J to **E**: A drink?

E to **J**: Shoperapy. Tonight @8.

E to **J**: You'll get your drink.

E to **J**: And I suspect much, much more.

Chapter 12: Ellie

Ellie waited anxiously, her new manicure tapping against a glass of champagne. It was all perfect. Just the way she'd pictured it. She'd arranged the shop's furniture in a circle beneath the pink chandelier. It was a safe space of rosy velvet, antique floral prints, and fringed throw pillows. A flickering chandelier overhead casts a warm glow, making the shop look almost magical. There were fresh flowers in the vases. Music played over the speakers.

The scene was set for a special night.

She'd spread the news of the shop's gathering far and wide. Posters around town, text messages to everyone in her contacts. She'd even had Chase whispering in the changing rooms at work. She hoped for a crowd, but she'd learned that enthusiasm wasn't all that was needed for success. She'd told herself all that day to keep her expectations low.

But that didn't stop her heart from leaping when the little bell above the door announced the first arrival. Ellie was surprised to see that it was Sophie, the receptionist from the gym!

"I'm afraid you won't find a dumbbell in sight," Ellie said, greeting her with a kiss on each cheek.

Sophie laughed.

"If I don't see a dumbbell ever again, it'll be too soon," she joked. But then she gestured toward her yoga pants and grey gym logo hoodie. "I feel so underdressed, but I came straight from work, and the flyer said that you'll be covering the clothes, so—"

"Yes, yes," Ellie said, clapping her hands together. "You're completely fine. Here, here, come with me."

Ellie guided Sophie toward the changing rooms, where she had a special table laid out with the evening's special attire.

"Take your pick," she said, sweeping her arm over a staggering selection of silk pyjamas.

Sophie shyly touched the hem of a pair of baby blue pyjamas with little leaping sheep. Ellie leaned in and nudged Sophie's shoulder.

"I figured the women of our community deserved a good night out, but there's nothing more fun than a good night in," she explained. "So why not both?"

Sophie bit her lip, hesitant.

"And I can choose any of these I like?" she asked.

Ellie picked up the pair of pyjamas Sophie had been eyeing and placed them in her arms before steering her toward the changing room.

"You deserve to be treated like a queen for a night, my dear, Sophie," she said, "whether you like it or not."

Sophie laughed from behind the curtain. Ellie caught her reflection in the mirror: arms crossed stubbornly, a happy smile on her lips. If she had to strong-arm women into treating themselves, she would. When Sophie came out in her pyjamas, Ellie had a pair of vintage heels waiting for her in one hand and a glass of champagne in the other.

It wasn't long before Jess, Grace, and Victoria arrived. When they changed into their silk pyjamas, Ellie did the same. Outside, the sun was setting, but inside, the fun was just beginning.

Another woman poked her head inside the store, clearly very unsure whether to come inside or not.

"Umm… is this the ladies' evening event?" she asked.

Ellie ushered her inside quickly, afraid she might otherwise run off.

"You're in the right place, love," she said.

"Eliza."

"Eliza, darling," Ellie said, grinning widely.

After slipping into her pair of pyjamas, Eliza joined the conversation that had been going on on the couches, sharing her story. She had recently moved from a small village on the outskirts of Edinburgh and recounted how she felt lost and lonely, as if she were suspended in time.

"But nights like this, surrounded by kindness and laughter, remind me that community is everywhere," she reflected thoughtfully.

Eliza's authenticity struck a chord with Jess, and they quickly bonded over their experiences of searching for connections in a busy town.

"Ladies," Ellie announced over the chatter, "the store is yours tonight. Try on anything you'd like. And the pyjamas are a gift." Again, the ladies were hesitant at first until Ellie started shoving gowns, blouses, and mini-skirts at them. They loosened up slowly, but surely as the evening continued. Soon, they started to share clothes, swapping pieces they had tried on.

Jess found herself wearing a stunning pair of vintage heels that Ellie could see, which brought out a new level of confidence for her. "You can totally pull off that style," Victoria exclaimed, and the laughter continued as other members of the group joined in with suggestions. It was as if they were all stylists for one another, encouraging each other to step outside their comfort zones.

The night progressed with discussions about personal style, but at its heart, it was about healing. They spoke about their scars, not just those left by relationships but also those formed through various life experiences. Together, they turned their heartbreak into empowerment, encouraging one another to embrace their individuality while providing support for their vulnerabilities.

At one point, Grace finds a beautiful blazer that she is convinced is too extravagant for her. The group rallied around her, insisting she try it on despite her hesitations. When she finally did, the silky feeling from the blazer enveloped her, but it was the kindness and encouragement she received that made her feel truly special.

"You're not just wearing clothes; you're embodying your essence!" Ellie exclaimed, making all of them laugh.

Victoria came out next from the dressing room – she'd put back on her matching silk pyjamas with extra fluffy slippers. This made everyone laugh when they saw the elegant Victoria wearing fluffy slippers.

"I already feel lighter, and it covers my arms," Victoria said as she took the glass Ellie offered. "I don't see why I couldn't wear this to my next business meeting."

Ellie laughed, "We should make it a thing. I've found it's very hard to feel anxious in silk pyjamas. And we could all do with a little less anxiety."

Out of the fitting area came the other women in silk pyjamas of their own that matched their unique personalities and styles. Jess was wearing a pair of animal print pyjamas with her new vintage heels.

"Do you think Adam could resist this?" she asked, giving a little twirl.

"How could he refuse the animal in you?" Grace purred, drawing laughter from the group.

Just then, the door of the shop opened once more. Ellie couldn't believe it. Grace introduced the newcomers: a couple of her friends from high school, Lucy and Beth. Ellie was happy to have them – she could already see the community of women growing, even if her sales hadn't begun doing the same yet…

Ellie offered everyone another glass of champagne, and the women all sat down. Ellie, who was now wearing a pair of red silk pyjamas and gold satin slippers, explained what she intended the night to be: a safe space for women to discuss love and heartbreak, to encourage one another, to give advice, pointing out how everyone there was at different stages in life and love, different ages with different goals, but how they could all learn from one another's life experiences.

At first, it was a little awkward – everyone seemed a little shy and unsure. Ellie could feel that the energy in the room was still hesitant, despite the comfy pyjamas and free-pouring champagne. She had to do something…

Ellie thought that if she expected these women to open up and share, the best way to encourage them was through example.

So, Ellie opened up about Jake – she told the women about finding him with his office assistant and how it was such a cliché. The woman was very sympathetic, but then she told a funny story (well, funny now) about taking his clothes and throwing them onto the street while accidentally hitting an ice cream van and then having to deal with a very angry owner and a very angry customer who happened to have a pair of Jake's boxers on his head and his shirt on his icecream cone. She not only had to pay for the customer's order but also buy a bunch of ice cream cones and chocolate, which she had to sadly (or not so sadly) eat by herself.

"It did help with the heartbreak, I suppose," Ellie concluded with a shrug, a playful grin on her lips.

It was clear at first that no one wanted to laugh so as not to be rude. But then Grace broke.

"I'm so sorry, Ellie, but that's just too funny!"

She couldn't stop laughing, and soon Ellie was laughing, too.

"It is funny!" she said.

At least Jake was good for something, she thought: making everyone laugh and breaking the ice.

After that, everyone else began to share stories. Grace recounted the tale of her recent heartbreak with Tim and admitted she didn't know who she was anymore without him. She spoke of the evenings she'd spent crying and how she was attempting to rediscover herself outside of the relationship, but that it was hard. Ellie could see how each word Grace shared resonated with the group. It invited other stories and allowed the women to transform from strangers to friends in a matter of moments.

Jess told them all about Adam and how she couldn't face work anymore after the disaster that happened the other day.

"I ended up in the maintenance cupboard!" she said.

Ellie knew she'd been close to tears that night. Tonight, there were tears, too, but of laughter.

"I was so bored, I tidied up!" she added, and the shop burst into even more giggles.

Victoria then shared the story of her ex-husband and his new, much younger girlfriend, the dancer who was only a few years older than her daughter, Rachel.

"At least she's studying in Spain," Victoria sighed. "She didn't have to see the train wreck up close. Plus, there's the tapas."

Lucy, Grace's friend, chimed in with her own experience, explaining how she had poured herself into her jewellery designing as a distraction from a painful breakup with her then-girlfriend.

"It was like I was reborn," she said with a grin.

"Fashion became an expression of my freedom. I went from being heartbroken to designing jewellery that made other women feel beautiful. You've got to find the silver lining!"

Her passionate story inspired Ellie, and she was sure everyone else. They all shared knowing glances as they commiserated over the struggles of love and loss.

The night ended, but not without the woman exchanging contact details with their new friends. They promised to meet up again, to continue sharing stories and laughter among the racks of clothing and in the warmth of the friendships they built. The sun had set outside, reflecting their brightened spirits as they stepped back into the world, feeling uplifted by a night that had started among strangers but ended with the promise of enduring friendship.

And Ellie even makes a few sales! It had been at the forefront of her mind earlier, the finances of Shoperapy. But it was now almost like an afterthought, the money she'd brought in. The night had been rich in so many more meaningful ways.

However, that didn't stop her from saying her goodnights, locking the door to the boutique, and immediately hurrying back to her phone and texting Chase about her success.

This is going to work, darling. I know it is.

Posted: June 12th, 2025; 11:52PM (GMT)

User: Your Fashion Ellie-vator

Subscribers: 81

Hello again, you gorgeous ladies… whether in pyjamas or ball-gowns, you're gorgeous. Just gorgeous.

I'm writing this after a fabulous night at Shoperapy.

Tonight, I opened my doors to an amazing group of women who came to Shoperapy to not only try on clothes, but to meet other like-minded women, and it was amazing to see the power of women in the community coming together and to share their stories of heartbreak. The younger woman listened to the confidence and experience of the older women, leaving feeling empowered with knowledge of how the stars-in-the-eyes kind of love can help the more cautious kind of love to be bold, enough to take risks.

The women who have learned the hard way to value themselves shared their wisdom, so that maybe others can learn from their mistakes.

If you missed out tonight, look out for my next open event, or pop into the shop and try on some stunning outfits. Maybe you might be the one getting your happy-ever-after.

Remember, life will continue to throw curved balls. It will sometimes be hard and sometimes complicated, but life will sometimes be wonderful. You just need to believe in you…

Love Ellie x

Chapter 13: Grace

Grace stood behind the counter of the ice cream shop, the summer sun spilling through the large windows. Each time the bell above the door tinkled, her heart leapt in her chest. It was a sound she had grown fond of, but now, when waiting for someone to walk through the door, it had a different meaning.

"Two scoops of strawberry, please," a child's voice piped up, pulling her back to the present. With a smile, Grace filled the cone, layering the vibrant pink scoop with a generous sprinkle of rainbow toppings that sparkled like confetti.

"Here you go, sweetheart!" she said, watching as the child's eyes lit up, momentarily pulling her away from thoughts of Everett.

As the bell jingled again, her heart raced. This time, it was an older gentleman, stooped but sprightly, eyes kind and twinkling. "Afternoon, love! Just the usual, please," he called out. Grace nodded, her hands busy as she prepared his favourite: vanilla with caramel sauce.

"On a hot day like today, it's the only choice!" he smiled, and she felt warmth bubble in her chest, a community spirit revived in the tiny premises of her shop.

"Where's your friend today?" Grace found herself asking the gentleman as he paid.

"Not sure, but don't you worry. He'll be in for his usual ice- cream before you know it." He smiled.

Grace smiled weakly, thanking him as he left, the bell ringing softly behind him.

The day carried on like this: a small stream of customers filtered in and out while Grace's thoughts kept swirling back to him. "He's just busy," she whispered to herself, trying to squash the anxiety washing over her.

As the sun dipped lower in the sky, lights began to flicker on, casting a warm, golden glow within the shop. Grace took a deep breath, refocusing on the present. She scooped up a vibrant blue bubblegum ice cream. The shop was filled with laughter and chatter, familiar faces enjoying a summer day, and for a moment, she let herself forget her worries.

But every time the bell rang, her heart would still flutter. She served ice creams, decorated with whipped cream and maraschino cherries, offering a bright smile to anyone who approached. With each customer, she crafted a moment of connection, finding joy in their delight. Yet, her configuration of thoughts always returned to the single person she truly wanted to see.

Grace continued to check the door of the ice cream shop every time the little bell rang. Her heart rate increased each time it wasn't Everett.

Between serving colourful scoops of ice cream, Grace couldn't help but keep playing with her new earrings. They were dangly ones, delicate and shimmering, catching the light each time she turned her head. Made of silver with tiny glass beads that danced like tiny ballerinas, they produced a sweet, melodic sound — reminiscent of wind chimes in a gentle breeze. Every time she touched them, it brought a moment of joy, a bit of happiness amidst the uncertainty swirling in her heart. The earrings were a gift to herself, a little something to boost her spirits.

Her new earrings were supposed to be a reminder to herself that she deserved nice things - that's what the women at Shoperapy said last night (nice things like the earrings, nice things like Everett, who is a gentleman, unlike a certain so and so in certain far off country…)

Grace smiled as she thought back on the night the women shared together, she knew it was something special.

Her friends had always been close, but she pondered the mixed feelings that had always accompanied her friendships with women. They had often been tinged with an undercurrent of competition. Something she thought had to exist between women. The expectations, the pressure to appear perfect, flawless, as if they were in a constant race against each other. But that night at Shoperapy, the walls of rivalry began to crumble. It was a revelation that female friendships could be woven with threads of support, solidarity, and authenticity. Women supporting women, encouraging them to take that leap.

Jess, Victoria, and Ellie showed her how female friendships could be something more.

As she adjusted her earrings, Grace felt their gentle weight against her skin. They weren't just adornments; they were symbols of a promise she made to herself. A promise that she would invest in her happiness and that she would allow herself to seek joy and beauty. The women, Jess, Victoria, and Ellie, each had their stories and struggles, yet they had come together to lift one another up. Grace thought back to that moment, the way the sunlight poured through the shop windows, illuminating their smiles, and turning scepticism into confidence.

Lost in her thoughts, Grace suddenly perked up. The bell above the door rang again. The sound sent a jolt of excitement through her. It was always the hope, the anticipation that Everett might walk in, the gentleman she had been secretly admiring from afar.

He was charming in a way that was both disarming and invigorating. However, as she glanced up, disappointment washed over her. It was just another customer, someone unfamiliar.

Grace cast a quick look at the clock – three-quarters way through her shift. No need to panic.

She settled back behind the counter, reminding herself that Everett seldom arrived this early.

Tonight, Grace had made a vow. If he came in, she would speak to him. No more shying away under the guise of serving ice cream, no more keeping her head down when he approached. She would engage with him, ask him questions, and maybe even flirt a little. Did she even remember how to flirt, she thought?

Her heart raced at the thought. The very idea of him asking her out sent butterflies churning in her stomach. What if he did? What if he had been gathering the courage all along? The thoughts raced through her mind. Would she feel as if she were betraying Tim? Tim, who, in her heart, still held a piece of her soul—perhaps he was forever her soulmate, even if their paths had diverged. Would moving on feel liberating or guilt-ridden? It was a tangled web of emotions she found herself caught in.

Each time she felt the familiar swell of anxiety, she toyed with her earrings, recalling the encouraging words the women had shared. "You deserve beautiful things, Grace. Don't forget that." The mantra resonated within her, providing the strength to allow her heart to open again, if only just a fraction.

As the minutes dripped by, she served scoop after scoop; families, couples, and children all came into the shop for their sweet fix, yet her eyes continually searched the entrance. No Everett. The universe seemed to delight in teasing her.

The bell above the door rang again… Grace got excited… but no. Still not Everett.

She stole glances towards the door, hoping each time it would be him stepping inside, his smile breaking across from his face. But time and again, it wasn't. A young family walked in, excited children bouncing on their heels, eager for a rainbow of flavours. An elderly couple followed, holding hands, their eyes sparkling with memories, while a group of skater boys swaggered past, helmets tucked under their arms.

Every time Grace gets nervous as her shift continues, she touches her earrings and holds onto the ladies' advice.

Time passed, ice cream scoop after ice cream scoop, and still no Everett…

Her boss was packing up to leave for the day. The ice cream shop closed ten minutes ago. Grace was sweeping the floors.

Grace looked outside at the boardwalk, searching for Everett. Her boss, a lovely woman, who had seen Grace grow from a timid young girl into a confident young adult, began packing up as the night wore on. "Those floors look pretty clean to me," her boss teased, glancing up from her work.

Grace offered a half-hearted smile, her gaze still lingering on the doors. "I'm just going to give the floors one more pass," she said, hoping to lure Everett in with her dedication, as Her boss understood. She was aware of Grace's quiet infatuation, a shimmer of potential romance that hung in the air each time Everett entered. With a sympathetic nod, she departed for the evening, leaving Grace alone under the flickering fluorescent lights of the shop. The silence enveloped her, broken only by the soft whir of the freezers.

Grace was glad it was Rita who was on tonight as she was so different from her narky husband. She still didn't understand how they were a couple, but it seemed to work. I guess it takes all sorts to make a relationship, and opposites attract, she thought.

After Rita left, Grace continued sweeping for thirty more minutes. No Everett.

With every stroke, a sense of urgency grew. What if Everett didn't come in again? What if she had been foolish to hope? Resolute, she placed the broom aside. The image of her earrings flickered in her mind. Beautiful, shiny, a constant reminder of what she should be deserving of—yet at this moment, they felt burdensome.

It was dark when she locked up, and she was so disappointed that Everett didn't appear. Today was the day, the day she was going to take a leap… for love.

She should go home. But Grace left her bicycle locked up on the boardwalk for a moment. She marched across the sand and, in a huff, threw her new earrings as far as she could towards the ocean. She didn't feel like she deserved beautiful things.

She was fed up with love. Done with it. It was stupid to even try again in the first place.

"Enough," she sighed, determination hardening her voice. The earrings splashed into the sea, the waves accepting them with open arms, and Grace started to feel regret. What was she doing? Of course, she deserved beautiful things and happiness. At that moment, as she stood facing the sea, she understood that the next steps would not come easy, but they would come with the strength she had learned from the women of Shoperapy. She had to hope there would be another chance for beautiful things, for new experiences, and ultimately, for Everett.

The night stretched out before her, full of possibilities, as she turned back towards the bike. She could always buy new earrings, or maybe, just maybe, someone would buy them for her, she thought.

Whatever lay ahead could be embraced with open arms and an open heart.

Chapter 14: Jess

The conference room was filled with the lingering buzz of discussions, the chaotic aftermath of decisions made, and shared plans. Jess sat in her chair, her heart racing with unsaid words and unexpressed emotions as the boss concluded the morning session. "Right then, team, let's regroup this afternoon. Remember to send me your updates," he said, and with that, the overhead lights flickered back on, chasing away the dim atmosphere that had wrapped around them like a thick fog.

As the projector's light dimmed, Jess's gaze fell to the stack of work files she clutched to her chest. She was gripping them so tightly that the edges threatened to crease, each crinkling a reminder of her anxiety. It wasn't just the meeting that had her on edge; it was the conversation she knew was waiting just outside the door.

When the others shuffled out, the room suddenly felt vast and empty, as if the energy had been sucked out along with them. Someone pulled up the blinds, allowing the warm, golden light of the early evening sun to spill inside the room, juxtaposing the fluorescent glow that had cloaked their earlier discussions. For a brief moment, Jess felt the warmth on her skin, but it faded as her nerves resurfaced like an unwelcome flood.

"Adam, could I talk to you for a moment?" she asked, her voice barely above a whisper as he began to file out with the others. The way she faltered almost made her regret the request, but she clung to the hope that this conversation might ease some of the tension she had been harbouring.

Adam turned, his brown eyes lighting up as he caught her gaze.

He seemed pleased, an expression of genuine interest spreading across his face. "Oh, so you are still talking to me?" he nudged her playfully on the elbow, the warmth of his smile almost making her forget the millions of thoughts swirling in her head.

Jess felt her cheeks flush, heat creeping up to her ears as she fought back an embarrassed laugh. "Well, I wasn't exactly sure how to approach you ..." she trailed off, biting her lip, feeling vulnerable yet hopeful.

"Come on, Jess, is everything okay?" he said, leaning casually against the wall, arms crossed, eyebrows raised in a playful challenge. "What's on your mind?"

At that moment, Jess realised that perhaps she had built the situation up in her mind far too much. She took a deep breath, allowing the sunlight to wash away some of her insecurities. "I just wanted to talk to you, you know? I've felt so off lately, "

Hey, it's alright," Adam interrupted gently, his tone softening. "I get it; we all need space sometimes. I just wanted to make sure we're cool. You know I'm always here to chat if you need to."

Jess seemed to relax slightly, the tension in her shoulders loosening as she let out the breath, she didn't know she was holding. "Thanks, Adam. I really appreciate it. It's just... I value our friendship, and I didn't want to make things awkward."

His smile widened, the warmth of his acceptance wrapping around her like a comforting blanket. "We're good. No need to stress. Let's make a plan for our next get-together."

"Absolutely," Jess nodded, feeling her confidence reinflate slightly. "Maybe we could grab coffee? Just to catch up?"

"Sounds like a plan," Adam replied. "You know how much I love my coffee."

As they stepped into the hallway together, the earlier awkwardness began to dissipate. The sun finally lit up their path forward, and for the first time all week, Jess felt a lightness in her heart—a glimpse of hope that she had almost forgotten existed, but she knew she still had to tell him how she felt. She had to be brave.

After a later-than-usual lunch, not that she could eat much anyway, Jess headed to the conference room for her final meeting of the day. No more postponement. She had to listen to the woman of Shoperapy and tell Adam how she felt.

As she sat down at the long conference table, the early evening sun streamed through the large windows, casting long shadows that seemed to mock her anxious energy. She glanced around, taking in the bland decor—grey walls adorned with monochrome prints—and felt as if the entire space was a reflection of her tangled emotions.

As Adam entered, she felt a wave of unease wash over her. His confident stride was a stark contrast to her own jittery demeanour, making her feel like an awkward child in the presence of a seasoned adult. He sat in his usual space, next to her.

"Hey, Jess. Can I ask you something?" he asked, his tone casual yet laced with sincerity. Jess nodded, forcing a smile that felt as strained as a rubber band ready to snap. The knot in her stomach tightened as she prepared herself for the conversation she had been dreading.

She could see the concern etched on his face—sincere and unwavering. It was as if he knew there was a weighty elephant perched in the corner of the room, one that Jess had been trying to ignore for far too long.

"Are you sure I didn't do something wrong, Jess?" he asked, his eyes locking onto hers with an intensity that made her stomach churn. She felt exposed, as if the walls were closing in, and the air grew heavy with unspoken words.

"No, no, of course not," Jess replied hastily, though the words tasted bitter on her tongue. She suddenly felt like a child caught in a web of her own lies, desperately searching for a way out. Her cheeks flushed with heat as she cursed her silence; she wished she could muster the courage to lay her feelings bare.

Jess was oblivious to what was happening in the meeting, but pleased Adam seemed to accept her response... or so she thought. "Are you alright, Jess?" Emily, her colleague, asked, lips stretched into a comforting smile. But the kindness in her voice felt like a spotlight, drawing even more attention to Jess's anxiety.

"I'm fine," Jess replies, forcing a smile that feels more like a grimace. "Just... thinking."

The atmosphere thickened around the room, heavy with the unshared truth that lingered in the air, and Jess felt a flicker of hope rise within her. This afternoon could become the catalyst for change—the revelation that might deepen their connection or, at the very least, free her from the unbearable weight of unspoken feelings. The conference room suddenly felt alive with possibility.

Thinking about the moment that lay ahead, she could almost hear the ticking of a clock inside her head, urging her to hurry. For a brief moment, Jess considered postponing telling Adam again. It really would be better at his apartment, or hers, where they could sit on the couch with a cup of tea, or at the park, sharing nervous laughter as the trees whisper secrets above them. Or on a trip down the coast, staring out at the waves crashing against the rocks, carving away at the shoreline just like her uncertainty gnaws at her resolve. But she shakes her head, trying to dispel the images before they seize control.

She stopped herself, feeling the weight of the promises she had made to the group at the ladies' night at Shoperapy. The clinking of glasses echoed in her mind, mixed with boisterous laughter as they encouraged her to be brave. "You have to tell him, Jess! No more hiding!" one of her friends had insisted, the passion in her eyes inspiring the others to nod enthusiastically. Jess could still see their approving smiles as they gathered to leave, a camaraderie that warmed the warm evening air.

Suddenly, the idea of retreat, of holding off on her news, felt disloyal. Jess remembered the sincerity in her friends' voices, resonating with the power of trust forged over countless late-night confessions. "You'll feel so much better once it's done," they promised.

And yet, here she was, trapped in a parade of fluorescent lights and whispers, knowing what she must do but longing for the comfort of solitude.

Adam, she reflected, would probably laugh at her nerves, if he knew. "It's just a conversation, Jess," he would say, shaking his head as if to shake the tension from the room. "You worry too much!"

But this wasn't just a conversation. It felt monumental, like standing on the edge of an expansive cliff, ready to leap into the unknown. The stakes felt high, and the thought of rejection loomed like a shadow over her.

Taking a deep breath, Jess clenched her fists at her sides. The cool glass of the conference room pressed against her back, solid and unyielding, grounding her. "No more running," she whispered under her breath.

"Jess?" Emily's voice came again, slicing through her thoughts like a warm knife through butter. "Are you sure you're okay?"

"Yeah," Jess responded, her voice steadier this time. "I just need a moment."

The gathered crowd began to leave the room at the end of the meeting, and their shadows flickered in the glass. She glanced one last time through the window, her heart racing. With finality, she decided.

"Alright, let's do this," she murmured to herself, collecting her things and making a beeline for the door. Today, she will take the leap.

She'd been so inspired by Grace's unfiltered, totally open, and expansive love for Tim (even if it was ill-fated and unwise…)

For so long, she'd thought love like that, call it puppy love, call it head over heels love, call it crazy love, was naive, silly, unreasonable.

But what the ladies suggested was that maybe that was Jess's way of protecting herself. By calling it silly, she never had to risk it. If she had dismissed that kind of love, she would have never had to get hurt by that kind of love.

In other words, the women at Shoperapy called her out: she was afraid.

She needed to be brave. And Jess was determined to be.

Right then. Right now.

Adam was looking at her funny. She could only imagine how her face looked, with all these thoughts and emotions going through her head.

'Jess, are you sure you're alright?' Adam asked.

When he reached out gently and touched her elbow, Jess did it. She jumped before she could think twice.

In a flood of words that she hardly understood herself, Jess told Adam everything. That she'd loved him since the moment they met. She'd always wanted to be more than friends. She thought they could be something really special together. That all she wanted was for them to give it a try, a real try. Even if it ruined everything, even if it crashed and burned, and their friendship didn't survive.

Adam was silent the whole time. And when she finished, he remained silent for a while, too.

Jess thought her heart was going to explode as she waited and waited to hear what he would say.

She was terrified, but it felt amazing. Having gotten all that off her chest. The women were right. This was the right thing to do.

Now, all she had to do was hear what Adam had to say about it all.

But in the end, Adam didn't say a word.

He opened his mouth. He closed it.

And then he turned and walked out of the conference room, leaving Jess completely and utterly stunned.

Chapter 15: Victoria

Victoria stepped out of the locker room, clutching her gym bag tightly as if it were a life raft. Her new halter-top gym shirt—an admittedly bold choice after a persuasive evening at Shoperapy—clung comfortably to her body. She couldn't deny it felt empowering, despite the way it accentuated her arms, her well-known area of insecurity. Just as she was about to strike a fierce pose in the large mirror by the treadmills, her phone buzzed impatiently in her pocket. After a quick glance, her mood plummeted.

"Cameron can't make it today. Great!" she muttered, rolling her eyes. "He's sent some good guy to step in. Just brilliant."

With a heavy sigh, Victoria tucked her phone back into her bag, wishing she could melt into the floor. Just as she was steeling herself to leave, she glanced up—only to freeze mid-sigh. Leaning casually against the treadmill, with a confident attitude shining out of him, was a very handsome man in a fitted gym shirt, exuding an air of effortless charm with a smile on his face that seemed to suggest he was aware of her inner turmoil.

"Are you Victoria?" his deep voice boomed, sending a few nearby gym-goers glancing over. "Cameron's made me aware of your training goals."

"Goals? More like grappling with my reality," she replied, forcing a chuckle, her confidence taking a wobbly step forward. "Is that so?" he grinned, clearly entertained. "Should I get the boxing gloves out?"

Victoria couldn't help but laugh in response, the tension lifting slightly.

Her heart leapt in her chest. It was too late to turn around and change into something more comfortable. The new trainer had clearly already seen her—yep, there he was, waving her over.

"It's just a training session," she murmured to herself, trying to sound convinced. "Nothing to worry about... right?"

It would be even more embarrassing to dart back inside the locker room. After all, she reminded herself, she was 52, not 16. She was a woman—one who was supposed to be confident and strong.

"Well, if I don't own it, who will?" she grumbled quietly, recalling her pep talk with Grace and Jess the other night, where they'd encouraged each other to walk into every room as they owned it.

Victoria chuckled nervously at the irony. "I might just own my nervousness, then!"

So, with a hesitant wave that felt more like a casual surrender, she began to walk over to the new trainer, even though she felt like she could kill for a shawl or cardigan at that moment.

The memory of her friends' encouraging words resonated in her mind. They'd made a big deal about how fabulous she looked during their Shoperapy night. "You've still got it, Victoria!"

Grace had exclaimed, while Jess chimed in, "You're absolutely stunning!"

Victoria wanted so desperately to believe them—that she looked fantastic. But the spectre of her ex loomed large, a shadow that had really knocked down her confidence. Each compliment felt like a lifebuoy thrown into turbulent waters, yet every time she tried to grab hold, the waves of doubt pulled her back under.

And there it was again, a reminder of her desire for a perfect 'revenge' body, a standard that was slowly proving impossible to attain. "Maybe if I just smile, I'll feel it," she muttered, trying her best to muster the confidence that seemed to elude her. She wanted so terribly to have this perfect 'revenge' body to get back at him that she might have set an impossible standard for herself.

The new trainer was looking at her expectantly, and she felt her cheeks flush. "Well, what do you think, Victoria? Ready to get started?"

"Ready as I'll ever be," she said, managing to return his smile, both sweetness and trepidation mingling in the expression. "Let's do this!"

Luca leaned against the gym wall, his bright smile radiating confidence. "I'm Luca, the new trainer," he announced, extending a hand towards Victoria. "Cameron asked me to tell you something important. He said it's a matter of life or death!"

"Is Cameron alright?" she blurted out, concern etching across her features, her heart skipping a beat as panic welled within her.

Luca, ever the optimist, saw the worry in her eyes and couldn't help but chuckle. His laughter was warm, igniting a flicker of hope within her. "Oh, don't worry! I'm pretty sure Cameron is just fine. Honestly, it's someone else who needs to be on high alert!" He swayed slightly, his playful charisma lighting up the gloomy atmosphere.

Victoria raised an eyebrow, intrigued yet sceptical. "What do you mean?" she inquired, leaning in a bit closer, her curiosity piqued.

With a cheeky grin, Luca leaned back against the railing, a mischievous glint in his eye. "I think it's someone named Ellie you need to be worried about!" His voice dripped with mischief, as if he'd just saved the best part of the story for last.

The name struck a chord deep within Victoria, sending a ripple of laughter escaping her lips. "Oh, boy... Cameron and Ellie?" she chuckled, the tension unravelling like an old wool scarf on a warm day. "This is certainly going to be interesting!"

Victoria grinned, her concerns for Cameron fading away into the friendliness of the atmosphere.

Luca stood by the weight rack, his laughter ringing out like a fresh melody in the bustling gym. "Come on, Victoria! You can't let those dumbbells outshine you! Think of them as your personal cheerleaders!" His playful banter continued, weaving through the air like the scent of fresh coffee. She chuckled, shaking her head. "Yeah! You know how it goes. A secret rendezvous here, a stolen glance there. It's definitely 'life or death' for the two of us!"

The gym was alive with the rhythmic clanking of weights and the energetic buzz of chatter, a tapestry of vitality woven together by the goals and ambitions of its occupants. Sweat glistened on brows, and the air pulsed with determination. Victoria, wiping the back of her hand across her forehead, grinned. "Well, if they're my cheerleaders, they'd better be ready for a show. I'll give them something to cheer about!"

A friendly competitiveness flared between them, solidified by their competitiveness. Luca waggled his eyebrows playfully, offloading a weight onto the nearby rack with a theatrical flourish. "Oh, please! You're the one who needs to watch out! I might just steal their thunder!"

A smirk played on Victoria's lips as she picked up her weights. "Careful, Luca. Remember, those dumbbells have been here long before you have." Laughter erupted again, drawing glances from their fellow gym-goers, drawn in by the infectious energy that crackled around them.

The gym echoed with their banter, a joyful interlude amidst the clanking and grunting. With each friendly jab, Victoria was reminded of her purpose: to not just strengthen her muscles, but also to ensure she keeps her revenge body. The session was kind of magical, she thought to herself, lit by sweat and smiles, affirming that sometimes, humour and revenge served as the best motivators in the pursuit of fitness.

As the two of them continued their playful exchanges, the bright fluorescent lights reflecting off the polished floor seemed to sparkle with promise. No matter how many times they slipped into serious competition, their laughter remained the thread that kept them united, ensuring that every workout felt more like a joyous celebration than a chore.

The gym echoed with their laughter, and for a moment, the weight of the world seemed to lift. With each set, Victoria felt a spark of energy igniting within her. Luca was a great trainer and infectious; he guided her through the routines with an ease that made even the toughest exercises feel like a dance. When he adjusted her posture, she noted the warmth of his hands on her waist. "Just a bit more of a bend in the knees," he instructed, flashing a grin that made her pulse quicken.

"Got it!" she exclaimed, her confidence swelling. He was funny, kind, and oddly perceptive, effortlessly picking up on the rhythm of her movements and her hesitations.

"I never thought gym sessions could be this much fun," she admitted amidst breaths of exertion. Victoria began to ponder whether this connection was the result of her newfound self-love. Was it possible that the girls were right when they said it's all about feeling sexy from the inside out?

With each rep she was made to do, Victoria could feel a spark of her old self breaking through—the capable woman who had taken countless risks and made bold choices long before her insecurities began to overshadow her. Perhaps the journey to reclaiming her confidence didn't require a 'revenge' body after all, just a willingness to embrace who she was, flaws and all.

"Is it common for trainers to crack so many jokes?" she asked between breaths, her heart pounding but her spirits rising.

"What can I say? A good laugh always burns more calories!" he shot back with a grin.

"Fantastic! So, I'll just be jogging on the laughter track then," she retorted, her eyes twinkling.

As their session continued, Victoria found herself leaning into the humour, encouraging playful exchanges. The gym echoed with laughter, a stark contrast to the heavy silence that had filled the room just moments before. "Come on, Marcus! Is that your version of a warm-up, or are you just trying to impress us?" she teased, her eyes sparkling with mischief.

The easy banter was infectious, wrapping around them like a warm blanket. As she listened to the back-and-forth, Victoria felt the tension in her shoulders ease. The self-imposed standards she'd clutched so tightly were slipping through her fingers, replaced by the joy of shared moments.

"Alright, team! Let's show those weights who's boss!" he shouted, grinning widely.

Victoria responded with groans of exaggerated effort, laughter crackling like static in the air. It was in this lightness that Victoria discovered a new sense of freedom. Encouraged by Luca, she realised that the weight of expectations was far lighter when working out with a great trainer, and being fit and handsome helped, too, she thought to herself.

Victoria was feeling great and excited at the end of their session. And then Luca dropped casually, saying that in the afternoon, he needed to remember to pick up milk. His wife had asked him…

Chapter 16: Ellie

It was an unusually blustery day in Meadowbank – bright blue skies and white clouds moved quickly overhead and not as unusual as the weather, another quiet, uneventful day in Shoperapy... again!

Ellie stood before her reflection in the sparkly shop window, dressed in a chic trouser coord set in white with moon and star print that hugged her curves in all the right places. With a dash of whimsy, she admired her reflection, half-seriously questioning if she looked more like a fashion icon from a glossy magazine or a hassled shopkeeper trapped in her own fashion fantasy. "Today's the day," she proclaimed softly to herself.

Tucking a vibrant stack of red and pink flyers beneath her arm, she paused momentarily to wrestle her rebellious hair into a sleek ponytail, her expression shifting to exasperation. "That's the last time my hair gets entrapped in my lipstick, thank you very much!" she declared, rolling her eyes dramatically at her own fashion mishaps. Perhaps hilarity was the only remedy to alleviate the day's stress.

With a burst of positivity, Ellie stepped out onto the bustling sidewalk to engage with a couple of women glued to their phones, seemingly more captivated by their screens than the fashion waiting inside her shop. "Good morning, ladies!" she called, her voice buoyant with enthusiasm. "Have you had the chance to visit the newest fashion boutique, Shoperapy? We've got a fabulous 10% off for all new customers today!"

One of the women looked up for a second, unsettled from her digital handpiece. "Oh, sorry, not today, but we intend to go soon!" she replied, her eyes sweeping over Ellie's outfit. "And I absolutely adore your coordinated outfit! Can I purchase that in your shop?"

Ellie seized the opportunity, her heart doing a little jig. "Yes! It comes in three fabulous patterns, and as I mentioned on the flyer, you can enjoy a splendid 10% off!"

"Brilliant! We'll pop in soon," the woman affirmed, her friend nodding emphatically as they strolled away, absorbed in their conversation. Ellie's heart plummeted slightly at their casual dismissal, that familiar pang of disappointment gnawing at her. "Ah, the nuances of Scottish hospitality—delivered with a scoop of longing!" she muttered under her breath, the irony not lost on her.

Ever the optimist, Ellie persisted, continuing to distribute her colourful flyers, the brisk wind playfully messing with her sleek ponytail, "Come on, you lot! Fashion waits for no one!" she declared, laughter bubbling from a few amused onlookers as her enthusiasm painted a delightful picture of spirited determination.

As she approached another group of women—this time intently focused on their ice creams—she summoned her courage. "Excuse me, are you all interested in the latest fashion trends? Shoperapy boasts the finest styles with an enticing 10% off for newcomers!"

"Thank you, but I'm currently indulging in this delicious sugar high!" a young woman replied, waving her ice cream cone like a trophy of victory over hunger.

Ellie couldn't help but laugh, her disappointment now mingling with a warm sense of camaraderie. "Fair play! But just you wait until that sugar crash hits!" As they disappeared into the crowd of blissful pedestrians, her spirits lifted again, optimism reigniting in her heart.

"Guess I'll just have to woo them back when their taste buds have recalibrated!" With her feet lightened by renewed resolve, she ventured forth on her promotional crusade, ever hopeful that amidst the sea of weekend revelry, someone would indeed be tempted to step into Shoperapy for an alluring bargain.

The flyers nearly went spilling onto the sidewalk when she just so happened to see a certain someone coming her way... Ellie managed to grab onto the Flyers, but it was close.

Ellie tried to ignore Cameron as he walked closer.

She continued to pass out flyers to people passing, continuing to tell them about her store, her purpose – all to promote her business.

Most people didn't appear very interested, and she just didn't get why – what was she missing?

She was a little flustered and frustrated when Cameron stopped right beside her, hands locked behind his back, rocking on his heels.

Ellie assumed he was mad about something else. What is it this time?

She's not sure what it could possibly be; she hadn't done anything bad (unless you count thinking about him all the time and not being able to get him out of her mind).

As she gave away some flyers, Cameron walked in front of her with a cheeky grin plastered on his face. She was surprised to see he didn't look mad at her... this time but said he was there to help her.

Ellie was stunned – help her? Cameron? The biggest grouch in Meadowbank? The man who seemed to have a personal vendetta against her? The very attractive personal trainer who had the nicest arms she'd seen in a long time? Help her?

No, this must be some kind of joke. She resumed passing out the flyers as he stood there, waiting for him to leave.

But Cameron insisted in his demanding, no-nonsense tone, 'Give me some of those flyers.'

Ellie glanced at him. He looked serious, his hand held out... like he was serious.

Ellie stepped back, amused and holding the Flyers tight. "Not a chance! These are my babies; I'm not just handing them out to anyone, you know. I need to ensure someone capable is responsible for the distribution."

"C'mon Ellie, maybe what you need is a strapping, good-looking, attractive man to entice all these women into your shop." He said with a twinkle in his eye.

"Do you know any?" she laughed. "No, I'm perfectly fine on my own, thank you very much."

Cameron gritted his teeth. "Even when I'm trying to help you, you're still just as stubborn as always."

Ellie got distracted from passing out the flyers – all those potential customers going by! Her sole focus was on not letting Cameron have any of the Flyers.

"That's the spirit! But no, my Flyers are safe with me. I don't want them to suffer under your 'care.'" Ellie laughed.

Cameron, trying to pull the Flyers from Ellie's soft hands, grinned, "You're surprisingly strong for a fashionista! Those sessions at the gym are obviously working."

"Must be the great instructor I have." She said sarcastically. They continued to struggle over the flyers when all of a sudden, Ellie wasn't even sure how it happened, Cameron was behind her with his arms around her.

She couldn't help but notice how strong he was. How nice it felt. How good he smelled... she was so caught up in Cameron's presence and touch that when a particularly strong gust of wind came through, she forgot to hold on tight to the flyers.

Just like how she imagined it happening, it happens. Cameron tried to take the flyers from Ellie, as she wiggled the flyers teasingly as Cameron lunged forward. The two of them struggled playfully, grabbing at the flyers, laughter spilling out uncontrollably. Cameron did indeed appear stronger; Ellie could feel the muscles ripple in his arms as they wrestled for control.

Suddenly, the flyers fell. They got caught in the wind and went tumbling down the street towards the beach.

"No! My flyers!" Ellie screamed.

Cameron jumped back, eyes wide, "I think your babies just declared independence!"

Both burst into a fit of laughter, kicking into high gear as they rushed after the colourful paper flapping in the breeze.

"I'll catch the pink ones! You grab the red! It's like the Olympics of flyer collecting!" Ellie screamed.

"I'm more of an all-rounder, come on! You know I can't resist a challenge! Cameron laughed.

Cameron and Ellie ran after them, each blaming the other as they scooped up as many as they could in their arms.

They continued diving around, dodging pedestrians and hopping over curbs. Ellie found herself breathless, laughing uncontrollably as the pair gathered the Flyers haphazardly. Cameron was slightly out of breath, falling against the sand after reaching the water's edge.

Ellie watched as her Flyers swirled in the surf.

Finally, after what seemed like a frantic eternity, they managed to gather them into a pile on the sand. Both fall on the sand in exhaustion.

Ellie, while gasping for air, "That was... well, a total disaster! But how much fun was that?"

Cameron lying down, chuckling, "Exhausting! And you were amazing. Who knew you were an athletic flyer-hunter like me? Maybe you ought to hire me for marketing."

Ellie leaning over, playfully shoving Cameron's shoulder, "Not with those skills. One gust of wind, and you'd leave me naked without my flyers! What would I do then? Besides, you still need to work on your running!"

Ellie noticed how strong he was, and he was quite good-looking, too, she thought to herself.

They looked at each other lying there, and it was very clear there was an attraction that neither could deny.

They both finally sat up, grinning at each other, panting slightly but beaming in shared joy. The tension between them was unmistakable, lingering in the air like a soft perfume.

"This was definitely more fun than moping around. Just you and I, the dynamic duo against the world—of flyers." Cameron laughed.

Ellie nudged him playfully again, "Indeed! But you do understand that I still refuse to let you handle them without further training, which might disrupt my fine establishment."

Ellie's eyes twinkled with humour, and Cameron couldn't help but smile wider, the warmth in their connection obvious. The short chaos faded as the sun began to lower, casting a golden hue around them.

"Fine, as long as I get to help again next time, I'll start training to be your official flyer distributor." Cameron smiled.

"Welcome aboard! Next, when I advertise on the radio, my ad will mention your strength! 'Cameron: the man who wrestles for cause!"

Cameron jumped up laughing and pulled Ellie up with his strong arms…. Ellie's heart beat faster as she felt Cameron's touch.

They both broke into laughter again, each stealing a sidelong glance at the other, neither quite wanting the moment to end.

Eliie headed back into the shop and quickly emailed Chase:

Dear Chase,

Um, you know how I kind of swore off love forever? Well, what if I maybe kind of wanted to give it one more baby chance…? Just this once! I swear…

Your hopeless friend,

                          Ellie x

Chapter 17: Ellie

Ellie couldn't help but smile as she arranged vibrant scarves on the rack. Outside, the streets hummed with life, laughter, chatter, and the distant sound of music from the nearby coffee shop weaved through the cool evening air. Today, two teenagers entered her store, giggling as they browsed through the colourful display. Their faces lit up in delight as they tried on hats and scarves, rotating in front of a full-length mirror.

"Hey, look at this one! I feel like a queen!" one of them exclaimed, and Ellie's heart warmed at the joy radiating in her shop, her smile becoming bigger.

Ellie moved over to the bag section and began to rearrange the bags by style while the soft chime of the bell above the door rang out as a few customers entered. However, even though she didn't want to admit it, the reason she was smiling today wasn't just because of the warmth and joy of her shop but because of something more personal. Ellie knew that it wasn't just the growing connection she had made with her community through her shop and blog, but the special connection she had made with a special someone, and she was sure he felt it too, that was making her smile today.

As she arranged the bags in a delightful display, her thoughts wandered to the day spent chatting with Cameron, chasing Flyers. Their conversation flowed effortlessly, a delightful mix of laughter and sarcasm. Since their paths had crossed, Ellie had felt more alive, as if vibrant colours had been added to the canvas of her daily life. Each time she saw him, he brought feelings that lingered long after he had gone, leaving behind a glow in her heart.

Yet, Ellie was also worried. Was it too soon to think about their connection in a deeper way? Would he be just as happy to see her as she was to see him? These thoughts fluttered through her mind. She had been hurt before, and the fear of vulnerability loomed large. Nevertheless, the thrill of possibility was intoxicating, urging her to take a chance with Cameron.

Closing her eyes for a moment, she took a deep breath, allowing herself to dream. What if they could create something beautiful together? What if their individual passions fused into something greater? No matter what lay ahead, she felt grateful for the connection they had made.

The two teenagers left full of laughter and hi-jinks, and as the door closed softly behind them, Ellie took a moment to breathe. With a heart full of joy, she thought to herself, how can I be this happy!

With a new sense of purpose, she opened her eyes and welcomed the next customer into her fashion shop, her heart light and full of hope. The familiar chime of the doorbell rang out, punctuating the soft murmur of the shop. It was a gorgeous sunny day in Meadowbank, and the vibrant colours of the new summer collection glowed under the warm lights, creating an inviting atmosphere that matched the weather outside. "Hello, welcome to Shoperapy!" Ellie beamed, her voice bright and infectious like a ray of sunshine. "What can I do for you today? Feel like a daring body-con dress or perhaps the colour of the season, yellow?"

The customer, a young woman wearing stunning oversized green glasses, chuckled softly. "As tempting as the body-con dress is, I think I'll stick to something more fun for now. One can only embrace the sexier look in small doses, right?"

"Wise choice!" Ellie replied, twirling a finger towards the rack. "We wouldn't want you to scare your dog when you arrive home!"

The woman laughed, glancing at the selection with renewed interest. As they chatted about styles and trends, Ellie felt the gentle flicker of excitement. Today was going to be good; she could feel it in her bones, and the shop was brimming with potential.

Later, as Ellie was arranging a few delicate necklaces on her shop counter, a familiar chime sounded, signalling that the door had opened. Ellie's thoughts were interrupted by a surprise visitor: Everett!

"What are you doing here?" she asked, her voice slightly higher than usual, as she tried to mask her surprise.

"I was hoping to find you," he replied, running a hand through his tousled hair. He looked the same, with those sparkly eyes that seemed to dance like sunlight on water, but he also appeared more serious — like a storm was brewing just beneath the surface.

"What do you mean you were hoping to find me?" Ellie stammered. Her mind raced back to what Grace had texted her, disappointment woven through every word. It had been a simple message: "He didn't show, Ellie. I think I've lost him for good." Ellie remembered how Grace's text had sounded as if the very air around her had deflated like a punctured balloon.

"Ellie, listen. I need to talk about Grace," Everett said, cutting through her thoughts. Ellie's heart sank. The last thing she wanted was to be stuck in the middle of a love story gone wrong.

"What about her?" Ellie managed to ask, her voice strained like a stretched rubber band ready to snap.

"She… she threw away these earrings. I'm sure these are hers. I've seen her wearing them in the ice cream shop." he said, placing a small velvet pouch on the counter. "I found them. They washed up on the beach today."

Ellie's heart raced. Those earrings had symbolised Grace's determination to move on — to let go of Tim and embrace something new. "You're saying she threw them away? Just like that?"

"Yes, I think I saw her on the beach last night. I went to the ice cream shop to see her, but I missed her, and then I walked home along the beach...I'm sure it was Grace." He paused, looking straight into Ellie's eyes as if he were trying to reach inside her very soul. "If those are indeed her earrings, it's a sign that I found them... It's fate, don't you think?"

Ellie picked up the earrings, a shiver running down her spine. They sparkled under the shop lights like tiny stars trapped in her palm. Ellie knew right away that they belonged to Grace.

There's no doubt about it: it had to be fate. Ellie knew what she had to do.

She had to get Everett and Grace together.

"He admitted that he had decided to give up until he found the earrings," he thought, despair settling like a weight on his chest. "Wouldn't anyone when it wasn't reciprocated?"

"You know these meant something to her, Everett. She wanted to be brave, but she's been feeling vulnerable lately."

"She has," he replied earnestly. "Do you think she still is? Can you help her, Ellie? Give her a nudge, maybe?"

With her heart pounding like a drum in her chest, Ellie contemplated for a moment. Grace had been so defeated, so convinced that love had slipped through her fingers. But what if Everett was right? What if this was the moment to rekindle hope and give Grace a nudge, a helping hand?

"Alright, I'll speak to her," Ellie finally said, her voice steadier now. "But you need to be honest with her, too. You need to tell her how you feel. Love is more than just bravery; it's about trust and vulnerability."

Everett nodded, relief washing over his face. "Thank you, Ellie. I just— I need a chance to talk to her and tell her how I feel."

Ellie smiled bittersweetly, recognising the weight of his words. "Let's see if we can make this happen."

Feeling as if the tide had shifted, Ellie knew something profound was about to unfold—not just between Grace and Everett but perhaps even within herself.

Ellie had been so disappointed when Grace texted her to tell her that Everett never showed up the day after the girls' evening at the shop.

Grace seemed so sad – she believed that he had given up on her, that she had missed her chance…

Grace had told Ellie that she was so frustrated that night that she threw her earrings right into the sea! She was done with love, just like Ellie! Ellie had it right.

As he looked deflated, the sound of Ellie's bright voice cut through his gloom. "Everett! Let's try again! I'm sure things will work out just fine this time." He sighed, running a hand through his hair. "Ellie, I so want this to be true, but how can you be so sure? I feel like a complete fool every time I walk into the ice cream shop."

Ellie's eyes softened as she observed Everett. She could see the shadows of doubt etched on his face; the confidence that once glimmered now dulled. "You're not a fool, Everett. Look, it's just a matter of giving her another chance to see how you feel about her. I know exactly what you need to build your confidence."

Everett looked confused, but before he could respond, the door swung open, and Chase, his usual upbeat self, walked in. "Hey, everyone!" he called out, shaking off the chill from the brisk Scottish evening. "I'm so glad to be off my feet after a long day at work!"

But before Chase could even reach them, Ellie was already pulling him back through the door, a determined gleam in her eye. "Chase, you're just the person we need! Everett needs a new look to reinvigorate his confidence."

Chase raised an eyebrow, chuckling tiredly. "What exactly do you have in mind?"

Ellie's excitement was infectious as she elaborated. "I've been thinking Everett needs something fresh, something that makes him feel good about himself. A haircut, maybe? A new style? We can go to that trendy place down the road where they really know how to work magic."

Everett stood there, still feigning bravado as he listened, but part of him stirred with a glimmer of hope. "You think that will really help?" he asked, his voice barely above a whisper. I really need some confidence!

"Absolutely!" Ellie said emphatically, nodding her head. "Trust me, nothing like a makeover to boost your spirits. You've got so much potential; it just needs to be uncovered."

Ellie leaned closer to Everett, a teasing grin spreading across her face. "Plus, you'll look fab! Grace won't know what's hit her." The excitement in her voice was infectious, making Everett feel a small flutter of anticipation within him.

As he gazed at his reflection in the mirror, the idea of a makeover felt daunting. He had always been the sort of person who blended into the background, never daring to stand out. But the thought of catching Grace's attention through a fresh look ignited a flicker of excitement in him. Perhaps he needed this change, not just for Grace, but for himself too.

"Makeover, Everett!" Ellie declared, clapping her hands together as if a brilliant light bulb had just illuminated above her head. "You need a style that screams 'confident and charming!'" Her enthusiasm was palpable, and for the first time, he began to envision what was possible.

Everett chuckled nervously, feeling both intrigued and terrified by the prospect. "What have you got in mind?" he asked, already picturing vibrant clothes and hairstyles that would make him feel exposed. He could almost hear Grace's laughter (not the cruel kind, but the genuine kind) instead of hiding behind his safe clothes.

"The works!" Ellie said, waving her hands like a conductor leading an orchestra. "We'll find the perfect outfits, a haircut that's daring yet classy, and maybe even some accessories! You'll walk into the ice cream shop and turn Grace's head, and the customers will be asking, 'Who's that?'"

With Ellie's encouragement and a dash of courage, Everett began to think that perhaps this makeover could indeed breathe new life into his confidence.

And turning to look at Chase, Ellie said with a huge grin on her face, "Chase, there's only one man I trust for the job! You are now Everett's personal stylist to reinvigorate his confidence and give him a makeover."

Chase laughed tiredly: 'Girl, good thing I love you.'

Chapter 18: Grace

Grace stood behind the counter of the ice cream store, meticulously rearranging the vibrant tubs of gelato as the afternoon sun filtered through the large front windows. The bell above the door chimed melodically, announcing the arrival of an eager customer.

"Hello there! What can I tempt you with today?" Grace asked, wiping her hands on her pristine apron, a hint of playful mischief sparkling in her eyes.

"I'll have the chocolate fudge brownie," the customer replied decisively, peering into the colourful array of flavours.

"Are you sure you can handle the chocolate fudge brownie?" Grace teased, raising an eyebrow. "It's a slippery slope into pure indulgence! Last week, I had a customer start with chocolate and end up ordering enough gelato to fill a bathtub!"

The customer laughed, imagining the sight of a tub full of gelato, and with a grin, said, "You know what? Perhaps I need a small scoop of the hazelnut, too, just to keep things balanced."

"Ah, an excellent choice! One for your taste buds and one for your conscience!" Grace replied with a wink as she expertly scooped both flavours and handed over the delightful creation with a flourish. "Here you go, your afternoon happiness, packed in a cone!"

A few minutes after the customer left, the bell chimed again. Grace looked up, her face brightened at the prospect of another visitor. However, her heart faltered when she caught sight of Victoria approaching. Grace blinked, momentarily startled, for

Victoria appeared dramatically different from her usual polished self but looked as though she had spent the night being chased by an angry bull.

Victoria, whose name was synonymous with elegance, stepped into the shop wearing oversized sweatpants that seemed to hide her toned frame. Grace's gaze instinctively dropped to Victoria's cuffs, and, to her astonishment, she noticed orange juice stains clinging to the fabric. But worse, Victoria's once meticulously styled hair was now haphazardly tossed on top of her head in a loosely arranged bun, strands rebelliously cascading around her face. The absence of her signature makeup flawlessly applied mask had been replaced by the unfortunate addition of a rogue smear of chocolate sauce across her lips.

"Victoria, are you alright?" Grace leaned across the counter, the concern in her voice laced with genuine trepidation, for it was unusual to see her friend in such a mess.

"You know, you're not exactly turning heads either," she shot back, her tone more biting than intended, a stark departure from the enduring warmth that usually radiated from their exchanges.

Grace paused to assess her own reflection, which had become increasingly unkind in light of recent events. Her sleepless nights had morphed into insatiable routines of scrolling through social media, lost in the maze of Tim's online escapades in Thailand—an obsession that had been highlighted more so since Everett had made a hasty exit from her life. Heat rose in her cheeks as she considered her own state; after all, she had dark circles under her eyes from sleepless nights thinking of Tim, or was it Everett?

Grace knew right away that Victoria was in pain. Grace recognized that kind of pain; it was the pain of the heart.

Grace said empathetically, "You look beautiful as always, Victoria."

Victoria smiled sadly. "Sorry for snapping at you. You look gorgeous as a daisy... as always."

The compliment, while genuine, hung in the air heavy with the unresolved tension of unspoken truths.

For a moment, both friends stood silently amidst the chaotic buzz of customers. There was a shared understanding of a bond forged through the trials of life recently—that silently echoed between them.

"Perhaps together, we could start a new trend," Victoria suggested playfully, allowing a hint of mischief to surface, her spirit momentarily buoyed. "I dare you to show up at your next Hinge date wearing these delightful sweats."

"Oh, please! I doubt anyone would swipe right after that," Grace replied with a playful roll of her eyes, a bright smile breaking through her previous gloom.

"Then perhaps a complete makeover is in order?" Victoria proposed an eyebrow raised mischievously, though her gaze still betrayed a lingering sadness. "When was the last time you let yourself shine to show everyone the magnificent person you truly are?"

"Honestly, I've been wrestling with burdens from Tim and Everett. It hasn't been easy to navigate this emotional fog."

Victoria nodded, the warm glow of empathy flooding her senses. "And I, as you can see, am grappling with my own array of emotional juice splatters."

The pair shared a knowing laugh while the ice cream store was alive, with customers blissfully unaware of the internal battles of the two-woman raging within it.

"Let's take a well-deserved break with an ice cream treat," Grace suggested with a glimmer of excitement rekindling in her eyes. "I believe we could use a splash of sweetness in our lives."

"Can I have a double chocolate cone to go, please?" Victoria asked with a smile.

"One, two, or three scoops?" Grace asked. 'Can you do four?'

Grace laughed. Of course, she could.

While making the cone, she glanced at Victoria, who was now hunched over the counter, lost in her thoughts. Grace could still see the flicker of discontent in her friend's eyes, a shadow cast over her usually joyful spirit.

"Earth to Victoria!" Grace called, tossing a playful scoop of chocolate sprinkles into the air, hoping to jolt her friend back to reality.

Victoria blinked, a half-smile appearing as the sprinkles rained down around her like confetti. "I'm going to need more than sprinkles to sort out this mess," she replied, drumming her fingers on the counter in an exaggerated rhythm. "Maybe a drum roll for my impending future could help?"

"It seems we both needed this moment—one of introspection and understanding," Grace offered, presenting Victoria with her cone, the gesture full of significance.

"Indeed," Victoria replied softly, the sincerity of her words enveloping them both. "Just because we're not at our best doesn't mean we're unworthy of the best that life and each other have to offer."

Their laughter echoed, genuine and warm, enveloping them in a cocoon of friendship.

Grace called out to Rita, who was the manager in charge, her voice breaking the silence, "I think I'll take my break now if that's alright with you." The tiredness in her tone was unmistakable, echoing her long shift spent serving customers. She could almost hear the kettle whispering promises of comfort and caffeine.

Rita looked up, her expression shifting from contemplation to surprise, and then a hint of relief washed over her face. "Go for it, Grace. You deserve a break," she replied.

Before slipping through the door that led to the beach, Grace scooped up an extravagant cone of her own, four monstrous scoops stacked high and wobbling precariously. As she turned around, she caught Victoria's eyes locked onto the avalanche of ice cream, and despite her heart's heaviness, a soft laugh bubbled from her lips. Grace's heart soared at the sound; laughter had always been the best remedy.

The two women stepped into the fresh sea breeze, crossing over the soft sand that gleamed under the weak sun. Grace looked sideways at Victoria, who had fallen silent again, her eyes tracing the horizon. They settled onto a soft dune, the rhythmic crash of waves below them creating a soothing backdrop to their conversation.

"I saw Luca at the gym today," Victoria began. Her tone was a mix of amusement and frustration. "You know, the married bloke with the killer abs? He just breezed past me, and I thought, 'What a mess I've made of love.'"

Grace nodded knowingly, shoving a spoonful of her mint chocolate chip into her mouth, savouring the chill that contrasted her warm thoughts. "What's wrong with us?" she prompted gently, her eyes encouraging her friend to share.

She sighed deeply, a sound laced with vulnerability. "I just feel like all the good ones must be taken. Honestly, Grace, what hope do I have at my age? Someone should have warned me how hard dating would be at 52, and yet, He (referring to her ex) can pick up a younger, fit dancer before his marriage has even ended. Life just isn't fair."

Grace reached over, resting her hand on Victoria's arm, grounding her in that moment. The café was bustling around them, with the low hum of conversation mingling with the aroma of fresh coffee and pastries. It contrasted sharply with the storm brewing inside Victoria.

"Victoria, it's never too late," Grace began, her tone warm yet firm. "The right person is out there; you just… you just haven't found them yet. You're incredible, and you deserve someone who sees that."

Victoria's lips twitched into a weak smile, a flicker of hope amidst the shadows. "You say that, but…maybe I'm just too much of a mess."

"Oh please," Grace laughed lightly, "you're so unbelievably gorgeous and unique. Like a limited edition. Besides, as for Him," she paused, rolling her eyes, "he'll soon see what he's lost. They all do. The grass isn't always greener, you know!"

The laughter bubbled between them, infectious in its sincerity. Victoria straightened up, the corners of her mouth lifting. The warmth of Grace's words had a magical effect, dispelling some of the chills of her earlier thoughts. With a bit of humour and conviction, she felt lighter; perhaps the world wasn't so bleak after all.

Victoria tilted her head, letting Grace's words sink in. There was a flicker of something—hope, perhaps?—crossing her mind. "Sometimes I think I'm overly picky, you know? Or worse, I'm not even sure what I'm looking for anymore."

"Maybe you need to be a bit reckless, then!" Grace suggested playfully, raising an eyebrow. "Throw caution to the wind! The world is vast, and you can find someone who brings out the best in you. Plus, think of all the ice cream we can have in the meantime!"

Victoria chuckled, the lines of stress softening around her eyes. "Maybe you're right. Life's too short to worry about what could go wrong. Perhaps I will take a risk or two."

She felt like the clock was ticking against her, as if she'd already missed her chance of love, happiness, and everything that came with it.

Grace's gaze fell upon Victoria, her new friend, who appeared to have breezed through life with an aura of confidence that Grace both admired and envied. She didn't quite understand how this beautiful woman could feel like this and thought to herself, "What hope do I have of finding the one?"

"Victoria, I feel like I've missed my window with Everett," she confessed, her voice barely above a whisper, tinged with self-doubt.

Victoria turned to her, laughter dancing in her bright eyes. "You're so young! Your window is a mile long!" Her voice was light and playful; she had this remarkable ability to lift Grace's spirits even when they were both knee-deep in their own insecurities.

Grace scrunched her nose in disbelief. "But you're older! You're more confident, more knowledgeable. You have everything—well, everything I don't. I can't even look at a nice guy without feeling... small." Vulnerability seeped into her words, accentuated by the way she tucked a strand of hair behind her ear, a familiar nervous gesture.

"Right, but let me tell you something," Victoria said, leaning closer, her tone earnest. "It's not about age; it's about believing in yourself. I've had my share of awkward moments, too. Look at me!" She gestured to her own clothes, stained with bright splashes of melting ice cream, an unintended distraction. "Confidence comes from knowing that it's okay not to be perfect."

Just then, a skateboarder who had been gliding past nearly lost his balance, his attention clearly diverted by the duo's lively conversation, or was it their outfits! He stumbled, and both women erupted into fits of giggles, momentarily forgetting their worries.

"Just think how we might attract men if we didn't have ice cream spilt all over us," Grace said, wiping a tear of laughter from her eye.

"Yeah," Victoria added, smirking at her friend, "whose idea was it to get so much ice cream in the first place?" The humour in their exchange lit a spark in Grace.

"But really, Grace, on those days when you feel shy or overwhelmed, just remember that it's okay to take small steps. You don't have to leap into the deep end of the pool right away. Start by striking up a conversation with someone you find interesting—see where it takes you and build your confidence." Victoria encouraged, her voice steady and affirming.

Grace nodded, her heart swelling with a mix of gratitude and longing. This was the strong, confident woman she now looked up to, the one who seemed to know how to paint the world in vibrant colours instead of drab shades of grey, like her.

Although Grace's clothes were also messy and covered in melting ice cream, complementing the bags under her eyes, she didn't care as much anymore. A different light lit her eyes, a sense of possibility flickering like a candle in the darkness. Maybe it was time for her to try to step out of the shadows that had held her captive since Tim left.

With a determined smile on her face, Grace looked at Victoria, who wore a hearty grin radiating positivity and strength. "You know what? You're right. I'll start small. Maybe next time, I'll talk to the guy when he comes in. If he can be brave enough to come to my work and try to talk to me, surely, I can take a bold step forward!"

Victoria clasped Grace's shoulders, her eyes sparkling with encouragement. "That's the spirit! I'll be right by your side. We can lift each other up, remember? Although I do think we need a visit to Shoperapy for some of Ellie's fashion tips before we take that step forward."

Together, they laughed, feeling as if their friendship could conquer any insecurity—even a mess of ice cream.

The sparkle of the late sunlight on the water gave Grace an idea as she picked up her phone:

Grace: You know those fancy dresses you have in the back…

Ellie: The ones with all the sequins…

Grace: And feathers…

Grace: And pearls…

Ellie: Yeah?

Grace: I think we'll be needing them…

Chapter 19: Jess

The last of the sunset had just gone down over the ocean as a big bonfire crackled and popped on the beach. Victoria had brought a cooler of champagne, the tracks it made in the sand still visible beneath the moon. In a semi-circle around the warm, glowing flames were four beach chairs Ellie had left earlier for the arrival of her three friends. The warm light flickered over the sand, illuminating occasional footprints that led to a cooler brimming with champagne, which still bore the tracks of the evening's excitement. In a semi-circle around the glowing flames stood four beach chairs, inviting and alluring, each occupied by a woman radiating elegance in their drop-dead gorgeous evening gowns.

Jess, draped in a mesh twisted Bardot evening gown in sapphire with gold fleck throughout and feather boa, epitomized her bohemian style with elegance, leaned back in her chair, a mischievous smile playing at the corners of her lips. The soft fabric shimmered under the moonlight, reflecting her now vibrant spirit.

"I can't believe we are sitting here together at the beach!" she exclaimed, her voice blending seamlessly with the rhythmic sound of the ocean waves. "It's such a fabulous idea, Grace. I am so pleased you came up with such an amazing plan."

"Absolutely! We should have thought of this before now," said Ellie, who sparkled in a pink dress that gleamed like the stars above. She took a sip from her champagne flute, her eyes sparkling with the same effulgence.

"Let's make this a night to remember!" Her enthusiasm was contagious, causing the others to chuckle and lift their glasses in a toast, acknowledging not only their time together but the journey, albeit short, that had brought them to this moment.

Victoria, a poised figure in a stunning emerald gown that flowed like the sea itself, leaned in, her expressive brown eyes shining with warmth. "I want to thank you all for being the incredible women you are," she began, her voice sincere and heartfelt. "Each of us has overcome heartache, and through it all, we're now here for one another. That's what true friendship looks like."

The sincerity in her words echoed deeply among the other women. Grace, adorned in a delicate blush gown that billowed softly around her, nodded in agreement.

"Ellie, you're now the glue that holds us together," she replied, her voice tinted with emotion. "I can't express how grateful I am to have friends like you. Each one of us lifts the other up."

With the warmth of the fire enveloping them, conversations shifted from past struggles to futures filled with possibility and hope. Ellie spoke of her ambitions for her boutique Shoperapy, her eyes sparkling as she envisioned dressing all the women of Meadowbank and beyond for their special occasions. Jess shared her accomplishments, recounting possible promotion at work. Their laughter and exchanged stories filled the air with a delightful blend of joy and inspiration.

"Let's promise to support one another in every endeavour," suggested Grace, raising her glass again, this time calling for a pledge. "Every time we celebrate a win, big or small, let's lift each other higher because we all deserve it."

They all looked amazing, like goddesses in the firelight. Ellie, in particular, looked stunning in her pink sequinned dress with its dazzling overlay for added sparkle and glamour. The flattering scoop neckline and sleeveless design created an elegant look, making it perfect for Ellie, the ultimate fashionista.

Jess laughed, warmth spreading through her as she took a sip of the Champagne Victoria had brought with her. Just a month ago, the idea of sharing a table with three new friends was as foreign to her as the concept of idleness. Workaholic by necessity, Jess had long allowed her career to dominate her life, leaving her without the connections that many seemed to take for granted.

Ellie had this enchanting ability to see the potential in others, no matter how clouded by self-doubt she might feel. As if she possessed a magical filter, she understood that beneath the layers of their busy lives, there were stories waiting to be shared.

Victoria had insisted Jess had to come, too.

"Alright, if you insist," Jess had said, fighting back against the urge to decline the invite.

Now, surrounded by her three friends, Jess began to realise how incredibly refreshing it could be to simply be in the company of other women who understood the challenges they each faced in their lives.

"Sometimes it feels like we're all carrying so much weight, doesn't it?" Grace said, glancing around at the group, her eyes filled with understanding.

"But when we share, it feels like we are lightening the load for one another."

Jess nodded, realising this was the heart of their gathering. As the evening unfolded, she discovered that sharing laughter, stories, and even a few tears created an invisible bond between them. It was therapeutic, lifting her spirits and igniting a spark of hope she had feared becoming extinct.

"That's it, isn't it?" Ellie chimed in, her smile like the sunlight breaking through clouds. "When women support each other, we become unstoppable." Her words resonated deeply with Jess, and she felt a warmth blossom within her as if each shared story was a stitch weaving their lives together.

Victoria came to understand that true empowerment flourishes in the spaces of women supporting women and sharing experiences. With a new perspective, she felt her heart brim with a renewed sense of belonging.

After their inspiring conversations and shared heartaches, Grace and Victoria stood up. It was time to do what they had come to the beach for.

As Jess sipped her champagne, Grace and Victoria unfurled a banner and drove two posts in the sand to hold it up.

Jess and Ellie both tilted their heads to read and say aloud, 'The Swear Off Love Forever Party.'

Jess laughed: 'Descriptive.'

Grace asked, "Is everyone ready?"

In their invitation to the party, they were all instructed to bring something to burn. A memory of an ex. A diary of past failed loves. An old T-shirt from the guy who never came back or who never became more than just a friend.

Jess felt that one in particular was directed at her. But it was true, wasn't it? Adam was never going to leave the comfort of friendship. He either wasn't brave enough, or she just wasn't worth it. Either way, Victoria offered to go first. Grace held her hand for support as she explained that she brought a business card.

It belonged to a very handsome, charming man. A new trainer at the gym. A guy with whom she could immediately see herself. A man who made her dream the second she saw him. A dude whom she was attracted to... revealed he was married.

The women all cheered when Victoria hurled the business card into the flames.

Grace was next. She brought a voucher for a free bag on an airline that flies to Thailand. She kept thinking that one day, Tim would ask her to come and meet him. But he hadn't. And he won't. So...

They all cheer.

Jess got up after a big, steady swig of champagne. It was her turn. The light from the fire dimmed slightly, casting a warm glow over the faces of her friends. A mix of emotions surged within her as she stood there, holding that little cocktail napkin in her hand, the faint smell of the bar still lingering in her mind. It was the cocktail napkin from the bar where she and Adam had gone after their very first day of work together, the day they met. The laughter they shared and the connection that blossomed seemed so vivid as if it had happened just yesterday. They had stayed far longer than intended, talking about everything from their hopes and dreams to the mundane details of their lives.

But now, Jess found herself at a crossroads. She really didn't want to get rid of it, but maybe it was time to let go of her feelings for Adam. She knew she was stalling a bit, caught between her feelings for Adam and the inevitability of change. She could almost hear Adam's voice teasing her about her sentimental ways. Could she really part with this tiny piece of their history? She took another deep breath, feeling the warmth of the champagne settle in her stomach.

Then, just when she had built up the courage, she was interrupted by a call.

She looked at her mobile and saw the name... it was... Adam!

Chapter 20: Ellie

'It's Adam,' Jess whispered, putting her hand over the mouthpiece on her mobile.

Jess glanced around the beach at the three-woman staring at her, her heart racing as she squeezed the mobile phone tightly in her hand. The soft flickering of the screen illuminated her anxious face, casting a nervous glow that reflected her uncertainty. "It's Adam," she whispered again, the words barely audible as she held up the phone. The whispers of her friends filled the air, growing more excited by the second.

"Put it on speaker," Ellie urged, her eyes wide with anticipation, a grin stretching across her face. In a heartbeat, the other girls chimed in, nodding fervently in agreement. It was a moment of community, a moment that tethered them all to the swirling emotions of life.

The women crowded together, and a small circle of support formed around Jess as she extended her arm, cradling the phone. Ellie, sensing Jess's apprehension, took the device from her shaking grasp. It hovered uncertainly between them, the connection to Adam hanging in the balance.

Grace and Victoria exchanged glances before placing reassuring hands on Jess's shoulders. It was a silent gesture, yet it spoke volumes. They understood what this moment meant to her, and they wanted her to know she wasn't alone in this.

"Hi, Adam," Jess said, her voice slightly higher than usual as she pressed the speaker-phone button. The unmistakable sound of Adam's voice crackled through the speaker. He sounded different. Almost strained, as if every word was a burden he had to lift.

"Hey, Jess," Adam started tentatively, "I'm really sorry for how I left the other day. I wasn't thinking straight." The regret was palpable, echoing in every syllable he uttered. The girls leaned in closer, their curiosity getting the better of them.

"Why did you leave so abruptly?" Jess implored softly, her eyes darting to Ellie, who looked as if she might burst with anxiety.

"I just... panicked," Adam continued, his voice wavering slightly. "I didn't mean to run off like that. I've been kicking myself for days about it. I haven't stopped thinking about you and what you said, and how I just... walked away."

The admission hung in the air, heavy with vulnerability. Jess felt her chest tighten at his words. The reminder of how he left her that day still stung.

"I was just so overwhelmed," Adam explained. "But trust me, I want to set things right. I miss hanging out with you, and Jess; I didn't mean to leave without telling you how I felt. I just... shut down."

Ellie, sensing the seriousness of the moment, glanced at Jess. Her gaze was filled with empathy, understanding that Adam's honesty was a step in the right direction for Jess.

"It's okay, Adam," Jess said gently. "Everyone has those moments. I just wish you had said something... anything!"

Adam's apology seemed to relieve some of the tension. Adam apologizes again for leaving abruptly, as he did the other day, without a word. He can't believe he did that. He had been beating himself up for days.

He continued to speak and admitted that he was overwhelmed by what Jess had said, her confession that she always saw him as more than a friend.

Adam admitted that he had no idea that she felt that way about him.

The women all looked at one another in the firelight from the bonfire, not sure where the conversation was heading. Jess was nervous.

Adam continued, "Jess, can we talk properly, not on the phone? Can we get together soon and talk?"

Jess mouthed to the others: 'What do I do?'

Ellie smiled. She remembers that feeling: the butterflies in the stomach from potential true love. The excitement of being on the verge of something special. It's confusing and scary, and there's no other feeling in the world like it.

They all mouthed back, 'Say 'yes'!' Jess looked to Ellie for her support. Ellie mouthed it, too. 'Yes. You have to say 'yes'.'

"Umm… yeah, alright," Jess said, holding back excited laughter till she said goodbye and Ellie hung up for her.

Jess was so overcome by joy and hope that she kicked off her very high, vintage heels, jumped up and down, and ran wildly into the sea. It was only a moment later that she remembered her dress.

'Omg, Ellie, I'm so sorry! I've probably ruined the dress!' (They're just on loan for the party.)

Victoria laughed and took Grace and Ellie's hands. They all ran into the ocean to celebrate.

The girls spent the rest of the evening discussing Adam's call, dissecting all that was said, the way women like to do. They all thought the talk was going to go well. They're perfect for each other – it was going to be love.

Ellie jokes, 'Maybe we'll have to change our sign.' (Which says, 'The Swear Off Love Forever Party') How about… 'Don't Give Up on Love too Quickly Party'. As they all laughed.

Ellie was secretly relieved that Adam called and 'ruined' the party. Because she really didn't want to burn the item that she brought as a representative of her dying love.

"Thank goodness," she muttered under her breath, glancing around. She had come to the party with good intentions, but every cheerful shout and clinking glass had felt like a reminder of her dwindling affection for the very person who had dragged her into this chaos.

"Ellie! Come on! Let's dance!" shouted Jess, who cut through her thoughts. Victoria, who was happy for Jess, waved her hands in an exaggerated manner, beckoning Ellie to join the throng of swirling bodies. But Ellie merely shook her head, her eyes drifting back to her purse, which seemed to weigh heavier with every second.

"Why did I even bring it?" she questioned silently, her fingers brushing against the cool edge of the poster tucked inside. It was a piece of art—or a statement, depending on how one chose to view it. The one Cameron had plastered onto the door of Shoperapy.

As the other woman continued to dance along the beach, Ellie stood rooted to the spot. Sneaking another glance into her purse, she let out a breath she didn't know she was holding. It was still there, waiting for her to make a decision.

Maybe tonight wasn't the time to let go after all.

She peeked into her purse. It was still there: the poster that Cameron put up on the door of Shoperapy, telling people not to shop there.

She didn't want to burn it, even if it was just metaphorical. The truth she was hiding was that she had feelings for Cameron, and it seemed like he had feelings for her, too. Because at the beach, he kind of asked her out. And she kind of said yes.

She had a secret: the woman who had fore-sworn love... had a date.

Blog post Posted: 6:33 AM (GMT)

User: Your Fashion Ellie-vator Subscribers: 78

A New Take On Love – Should We Be Giving Up On Love So Soon!

Good morning, you! Yes, you, gorgeous females! It's time to jump out of bed and seize the day...

Over the past few days, I've been rethinking the curious spectacle that is modern dating — I've come to realise something that fills me with equal parts hope and despair: the importance of not giving up on love too soon. A topic oh-so-serious.

Now, I know what you might be thinking: "But what if the chemistry is off? Shouldn't we just cut our losses and move on before it gets too messy?" While that's perfectly understandable (and highly relatable), here's the thing: love isn't always instantaneous fireworks and heart-shaped confetti. Sometimes, it's more a slow-burning candle or a misinterpreted grouchy man. And the trick is not to throw in the towel too soon, even when our first impressions make us want to run for the hills.

Before you close the door that says, "Do Not Open," I've realised that the one thing we must recognise in love is vulnerability is a strength, not a weakness. Each disastrous moment can lead to a treasure trove of lessons; each cringe-worthy experience is a stepping-stone towards that elusive "real thing."

And let's not forget the idea of "The One." Ah yes, that crazy notion that there's a perfect soul mate out there just waiting for us to find them. But what if, instead of seeking perfection, we let ourselves be vulnerable to imperfect people?

So, here's my challenge to you… gorgeous women: the next time you find yourself skeptical about love after a few hiccups, remember that it may just be the universe's way of highlighting the beautiful messiness of life. I urge you to stop swiping those dating apps in a frenzy. Instead, take a deep breath, turn up your favourite Spotify playlist of power ballads, and look for love in the most unexpected places. You might just find something worth hanging onto.

No matter how chaotic, cringe, or complex it may seem, love may actually be worth it. And who knows? You might just inspire someone else not to close the door to their heart before their next big love adventure begins.

On that note, I'm off to get some coffee in me and… seize the day.

Remember to pop into Shoperapy on Skyler Street and say 'hello,' and you might find that perfect outfit for that not-so-perfect date.

See you all soon!

Love,
Ellie x

Chapter 21: Victoria

Victoria settled onto a high metal stool at the sleek wooden counter of the café, her heart thrumming with a mix of excitement and nerves. The café had become a local favourite, famous not just for its aromatic coffee but also for its vibrant atmosphere. The high ceilings, exposed brick walls adorned with local artwork, and cascading plants created an enriching backdrop for life in Scotland. Neon signs glowed in the dim light, casting a kaleidoscope of colours onto the floor, complementing the youthful energy that buzzed through the air. Young people hustled behind the counter, their laughter blending with the hiss of the espresso machine, and for a moment, Victoria felt as though she belonged.

It wasn't long ago that the thought of working at a café surrounded by so many trendy individuals would have made Victoria's stomach twist in knots. In her mind, she often thought of her own perceived shortcomings—she wasn't 'hip' enough, didn't have the latest fashion, and certainly felt too old compared to the vibrant crowd that filled the space. As a freelance editor, she spent her days wrapped up in books and manuscripts, spinning words into a coherent tapestry while the outside world carried on without her. But not today, she reminded herself with a spark of determination. Thanks to Ellie, Victoria was wearing a stunning ensemble from her boutique, Shoperapy.

The outfit was a striking combination that suited her perfectly. The high-waisted trousers in deep forest green hugged her silhouette in all the right places, and the light, breathable top in soft cream fluttered gently around her arms. A delicate necklace from her daughter hung loosely around her neck, which added an air of elegance without feeling overdone. For the first time in weeks, she felt that familiar flutter of confidence. On her way to the café, she'd glanced at her reflection in a shop window and couldn't help but smile. She was no longer just a freelance editor; she was Victoria, a woman who could strut into a café and claim her space amongst the cool crowd.

As she opened her laptop, Victoria noticed that she was no longer just observing the lively chatter around her. She found herself relaxing in the ambience, engaging with the people around her, her laughter mingling with theirs. The insecurities that had plagued her just minutes earlier faded into the background, and she caught herself smiling at how refreshing it felt to embrace the moment without worrying about what others might think.

Feeling the call of nature, Victoria excused herself and made her way to the restroom. As she washed her hands and took a moment to collect her thoughts, she reminded herself that today was about embracing life – and she was determined to live it fully. When she returned to her seat, she stopped in her tracks, her heart skipping a beat. There lay a crisp white napkin on her keyboard. Curiosity piqued, she walked over and picked it up. There, in neat, flowing handwriting were the words,

Hi there. I just wanted to say I think you're absolutely gorgeous and would love to get to know you.

Instantly, a rush of warmth flooded through her, and she couldn't stop a grin from spreading across her face. Was this romantic note a playful jest or an Act of Devotion? In that moment, the note transformed her day into something magical. Victory felt a thrilling rush of possibility. She hadn't just made it through the café crowd; she had inadvertently attracted the attention of a stranger just by being herself.

In the dim light of the café, surrounded by laughter and the intoxicating aroma of coffee, Victoria took a moment to revel in her newfound confidence. With the napkin clutched tightly in her hand, she felt as if she had stepped into a new chapter of her life. Perhaps there was more to this youthful café scene than she had realised. It wasn't about age or fashion; it was about the energy each person brought to the table. For the first time in a long while, she felt alive, ready to take her place in the world, insecurities be damned.

With a flick of her wrist, she tossed the napkin down beside her drink, allowing the thrill of the unexpected to nestle comfortably in her heart. It was in that moment, cradling her coffee cup and surrounded by the clatter of cups and the laughter of people, that Victoria understood she was not just a freelance editor but part of a vibrant tapestry of life, rich with stories, laughter, and connections yet to be made.

Victoria was in the groove – not worrying about what people were thinking of her.

She felt her cheeks warming. She hadn't felt that in a long time.

It even felt good to be nervous!

She felt a little shy, keeping her focus on her screen, but there was no way that she was getting any further work done that afternoon. Slowly but surely, Victoria started glancing as subtly as she could around the cafe.

She looked over at a lot of people, but everyone seemed to be immersed in their work. She didn't catch anyone's eye. So, who was it? Who wrote that note?

Had he already left? Had she missed her chance? She'd just helped

Grace with this same issue, but there she was, worried she'd been too shy!

Victoria started to panic a little when she saw someone she'd missed before. He smiled at her. A very charming, lovely smile. Tan skin, toned arms, a nice suit. And he was smiling, yes, there's no denying it, he was smiling at her!

The only problem: It was the trainer. The new one. From the gym. The new trainer from the gym was MARRIED.

Victoria glanced around the bustling café; the noise of clinking cups and chatter felt like an annoying background track to her thoughts. Ugh! Are you kidding me? she mused, unable to shake off the cloud of irritation that settled on her shoulders. What was wrong with guys these days? It was as if basic decency had been lost somewhere between the last social media trend and the endless scrolling of mindless content.

She plastered on a polite, albeit fake, smile as a way to mask her inner turmoil. The Barista, oblivious to her frustrations, handed over her frothy cappuccino, perfectly crafted with a heart-shaped design emblazoned on the foam. Victoria crinkled her nose at it, feeling the flutter of annoyance surge again as she searched through her purse for something – anything – to channel her feelings onto. She took out the first piece of paper she could find – a faded receipt from her most recent purchase at Shoperapy.

In frustration, she retrieved a pen from her bag and began to write a note on the back of the slip. Her handwriting, usually neat and crisp, felt hurried and slightly jagged as her thoughts poured out. She scribbled her message before contemplating the ink's permanence on the flimsy receipt. No turning back now.

Once she had tucked the receipt into her clutch, Victoria took a deep breath, stealing herself before gathering her laptop and bag. Today was not about dwelling on the disappointments of the past; it was about moving forward. She made her way towards the personal trainer. He was still smiling, his grin fixed in place, and he had no idea how insulting he was.

Victoria mirrored his smile, though inside, she was still seething. What did he think this was – a game? She closed the gap between them with a light-hearted, almost playful stride that belied the storm raging within her. As she approached, she couldn't help but notice how surprisingly sharp he looked in his tailored jacket. Kind of dressed up for a personal trainer, she thought, shaking her head slightly at the absurdity of it.

With a flick of her wrist, she playfully tucked the receipt, adorned with her scrawled message, into his jacket pocket. She felt a mischievous thrill as it slid into place, a negligible act of defiance against the unwarranted attention he had thrust upon her. "Cheers!" she said cheerily, all while suppressing the urge to roll her eyes at the absurdity of the exchange.

With her heart racing from the blend of annoyance and excitement, Victoria stepped away from him, her façade of calm holding firm even as she felt a small thrill of satisfaction. She clutched her cappuccino tightly, the warmth in her hands a stark reminder that this moment, however fleeting, had simply been part of her journey. With one last glance over her shoulder at Him, she pushed the café door open and walked into the fresh air, ready to take on whatever the world had in store.

She didn't look back to watch him read it. She could guess his reaction. She didn't care. He deserved it for hitting on her when he was married. And when she knew that he was married.

Victoria really was done with love. Really this time! And what did the note say?

Get lost, loser!

Not that Victoria felt like the winner. No, there were no winners here.

She walked out of the café and over to the beach and sat on a bench to gather her thoughts... and calm down!

Taking out her phone to WhatsApp, the girls with the latest update, she noticed a few notifications from work, and then suddenly, like magic, a notification flashed from Ellie's Shoperapy Instagram. She pressed the notification to read the comment...

First Comment on Blog:

'To the beautiful woman I saw in the café who apparently shops at this shop: I meant no harm. I apologize if I offended you. - Levi' There was no denying that this was meant for her... but Levi?

She texted Cameron:

Victoria: I thought the trainer's name was Luca?

Cameron: It is.

Victoria: Then, who is Levi?

Cameron: His twin.

Cameron: Aunt Vic?

Cameron: Hello?

Cameron to Victoria: Hellooooo?

Chapter 22: Jess

Jess stood in front of her mirror, giving herself a pep talk as she scrutinised her reflection. "You've got this, Jess. Just breathe," she muttered, trying to sound more convincing than she felt. But deep down, she knew that no amount of self-encouragement could squash the nerves rumbling in her stomach.

The anticipation was overwhelming. Even the lengthy presentations at work—where she had to stand up in front of management—seemed trivial compared to what lay ahead. And those job interviews? A walk in the park compared to this excruciating wait. It was just a talk with Adam, for goodness' sake, but it felt as if she were preparing for a royal audience.

Jess paced her room—back and forth, back and forth—her palms were clammy, and her heart raced like it was training for the Olympics. She could almost hear the perpetual thumping in her chest, competing with the faint ticking of the clock on her wall. How was it possible that tonight was the night…the talk.

"What will he say?" she wondered, biting her lip. Then came the big questions: "Will he say he's always loved me, too? Or will he just apologize for everything and leave me with my heart in pieces?"

Jess glanced down at her watch. "I have to get a grip," she said, forcing herself to sit. Closing her eyes, she took a few deep breaths. "Just think rationally. It's just a chat." But rationality felt miles away.

As she glanced at the clock, she couldn't shake the laughable irony of her situation: all those years spent preparing for exams and interviews hadn't prepared her for this. Tonight was more than a 'what if'; it was a life-altering conversation with a friendship that meant so much to her.

Jess stood in her bedroom, surveying the array of outfits sprawled across her bed. From a sleek black dress to a floral skirt that fluttered with whimsy, she had meticulously selected each piece for what had become the most anticipated event of her week. With her hand resting thoughtfully on her chin, she pondered which outfit would shout 'fabulous' without saying a word.

She sent photos of her outfits to Ellie, seeking her stamp of approval. Jess valued Ellie's opinions more than she cared to admit; her friend was the ultimate fashionista and knew exactly what to wear for each occasion. Checking her phone for yet another notification, Jess felt her heart flutter again.

"Perfect!" the screen lit up like Ellie's cheerful enthusiasm. Jess could almost hear her friend's excited voice ringing in her ears. She chuckled at the thought of Ellie bouncing around her flat, a flurry of energy dressed in her trademark style.

One by one, Ellie's responses filled Jess's screen. "You'd look stunning in that!" echoed through her mind as she imagined herself in a sleek, red number that would hug her curves in all the right places. But then there was the vibrant sundress that Ellie had labelled, "Wow, amazing. Choose that one!" It was flowy and fun, perfect for swaying gently as she and Adam shared laughter together.

"Why is choosing an outfit for date night so complicated?" Jess mused aloud, a smile playing on her lips. She glanced at the ceiling, weighing her options like a courtroom judge. Would Adam prefer the elegance of simplicity, or would he enjoy the vibrant charm of the sundress?

But, as Jess looked them all over a second time, she really wasn't sure. One outfit screamed too girly, one screamed too worky, and one screamed not fancy enough. They're really not right – not any of them.

Jess shoved them off the side of her bed and rummaged through her wardrobe for more options. She took more pictures and sent Ellie more texts.

Jess tapped her foot, waiting for Ellie's thoughts. But instead of a text, Jess got a call. I'll answer that later, she thought.

Ellie was kind and gentle and assured Jess that whatever she chose, she would look great.

Ellie text! Think about it – on all those other dates you went on with guys, did you put this much effort into choosing your outfit?

Jess texted no, I didn't really go on dates, well, not with anyone who really mattered: there's only ever been one guy… Adam!

Ellie was stunned - what about guys in college?

Jess texted: nope - I've never felt about anyone the way I feel about Adam.

Jess knew it was risky - putting so much hope into one guy - Ellie didn't have to say it; she knew, too. The likelihood was that she would crash and burn with Adam, but she hoped this wouldn't be the case.

Ellie was kind as always: "No matter what happens, I'll be there for you. Now, let's pick you the perfect outfit. Send me the new options you put on the bed."

"Okay, okay! I'll choose," Jess laughed to herself, her confidence restored. With a deep breath, she picked up the sundress, letting it float down from her fingers like a butterfly settling onto a flower. "Ellie, you're right. This is the one!"

Jess hung the dress up on the door of her wardrobe and started to tidy her bedroom, her heart racing with an odd mix of excitement and dread. The room now an explosion of clothes, shoes, and assorted accessories.

Jess looked one more time at the dress that hung on the door of her wardrobe, letting it sway gently as if it were dancing to its own rhythm. "There you go, you lovely thing," she murmured, admiring the way the fabric caught the light. She appreciated the delicate lace trim that framed the neckline and the way the skirt flared out like a blooming flower. If only tidying was as much fun as wearing that dress would be, she thought!

With every bit of clothing that found its way to the wardrobe, Jess felt lighter. The warmth of the sunlight grew stronger, illuminating her transformation from an explosion of clothes into something vibrant, much like the dress hanging on her wardrobe door.

After what felt like hours but was probably more like a longer-than-usual coffee break, Jess stepped back to admire her handiwork. The room was revitalised. Her wardrobe was neatly organised, the shoes were stacked perfectly, and her bed and floor were finally visible again.

With a sigh of contentment, Jess fell on her bed, enjoying the now neatness of her bedroom, laughing at the mess she had created earlier… all because of her talk with Adam.

Ellie's final message lit up the screen, "Good luck, not that you'll need it. Can't wait to hear all about it! You're going to knock Adam off his feet!"

As she smiled at Ellie's text, the doorbell rang, stopping her in her tracks.

Startled, she leapt up, her mobile flying to the other side of the room. "What on earth?!" she gasped, stumbling to her bedroom window. As she glanced out the window, she felt sick. No, it couldn't be, could it?

Her heart raced. OMG, what does she even look like? Pyjamas? Check. Hair like it had been through a tornado? Double check. No makeup? Well, there you go, an emphatic triple-check! She could feel the blush creeping up her cheeks and cursed silently. "Not like this, not like this!"

She picked up her mobile and walked to the door... with absolutely no intention of opening it. Not looking like this!

"Umm... Jess?" a familiar voice emanated from the other side of the door, soft but laden with anticipation.

Who is it? A wave of dread washed over her as she realised it was Adam. Of course! It had to be the guy who made her stomach twist into creative knots. Jess pressed herself against the door like it might suddenly sprout legs and whisk her away to the land of Pyjama Freedom. She noticed the little peephole staring back at her and instinctively ducked as though she were hiding from some sort of monster.

Jess stood frozen in the narrow hallway of her apartment, her heart thumping like a drum in her chest. She could see the little peephole in the heavy wooden door—its black circle staring back at her like the eye of a monster, waiting to pounce. Instinctively, she ducked, pressing her back against the cool wall as if it could shield her from the impending confrontation with Adam.

"Jess?" came the voice on the other side moments later. Adam's tone was cautious, laced with uncertainty, as he called her name once more. "I—I just couldn't wait to talk to you." The warmth of his voice contrasted sharply with the chill that ran through her.

Crumpling down onto the floor, Jess slid helplessly to a seated position, her hands instinctively covering her face like a shield. What now?! She thought desperately, weighing her options. Did she gather her courage and face Adam in this mess, even if he had only ever seen her dressed to perfection, or was it easier to pretend she hadn't heard him.

Taking a deep breath, she untangled her fingers from her hair and peeked through the peephole, her heart racing. There he was, Adam, his hair slightly tousled the way she liked it, his brow furrowed in concern. His navy blazer, a familiar sight, hugged his frame just right, the familiarity making him appear less intimidating and more approachable.

"What if he thinks I'm hiding?" she mused, her mind racing. "What if he just walks away?!" The thought sent a shiver down her spine, and Jess gritted her teeth, forcing herself to respond before she lost her chance.

This was not how she had envisioned their chat…

Taking a deep breath, Jess considered her options. 'Just be yourself,' she thought. Slip past the embarrassment and let the potential for an awkward yet much-needed chat unfold. After all, her confidence might well improve when Adam started to talk, even if her hair certainly would not.

Taking her phone from her Pyjama pocket… she texted Ellie…

Jess to Ellie: Adam's here! What do I do?!!! (*Message unread*)

Chapter 23: Grace

Grace said goodnight to her boss. It was her turn to clean up and close the ice cream shop.

The shop fell silent as Grace flipped the sign from 'OPEN' to 'CLOSED,' the jingle of the bell above the door fading into the backdrop of soft, lingering thoughts. It was her turn to clean up, and though the air was filled with the sweet aroma of vanilla and sprinkles, her heart had danced to a different tune not long ago.

Nights like this used to fill her with dread. Alone and surrounded by fading memories of laughter and chatter, Grace would often lose herself in thoughts of Tim. The quiet would creep around her, pressing down like an unwelcome blanket, making her reach for her phone every five minutes, desperately waiting for a message that never came. Those moments had dragged on until well past midnight, her tasks growing heavier with each tick of the clock as she clung to the hope that his name would light up her screen.

But tonight felt different. With each sweep of the broom, she could feel a sense of liberation fill the air. Grace had discovered a newfound strength within herself. The chains of anxiety linked to Tim had loosened like a spell finally breaking after an eternity. She smiled to herself, humming a little tune that danced through her mind—an upbeat melody she cherished by Viola Wills: 'I'm gonna get along without you now,' a tune Tim would have dismissed as 'not cool enough' but which she loved and felt was perfect for how she was feeling.

As Grace swept the floor, she could almost hear the tunes of her favourite songs filling the space, connecting memories of carefree afternoons with friends rather than worries about what someone else thought. She moved to the rhythm, her body swaying as she hummed notes of freedom and self-acceptance. The shop transformed into her personal stage, each motion a celebration of her independence.

But even though things didn't work out with Everett—Grace felt surprisingly at ease. The cobwebs of anxiety that used to wrap tightly around her heart when she thought of Tim were slowly disintegrating. It felt as though a spell had been broken; the chains of worry were falling away, piece by piece, and she could finally breathe again.

With a lightness in her step, Grace began to hum another of her favourite tunes from her favourite indie band, a sweet melody that had always brought her comfort—the kind of music she adored, with jangly guitar riffs and uplifting lyrics but which Tim never allowed her to play when he was around. He scoffed at her taste, declaring it too 'cheesy' and 'not cool.' What did he know? A good tune was like a warm blanket on a chilly night, and today, she wrapped herself in her beloved sounds, unfurling them to fill the shop.

As she hummed her heart out, Grace didn't notice the gentle chime of the bell above the door as a figure stepped inside the shop, nor did she catch the amused smile playing across their lips. Thirty minutes earlier, she had flipped the 'CLOSED' sign, yet here she was, caught up in her own little world, blissfully unaware of the person who had walked into the shop. Perhaps it was her dulcet tones they heard from outside; she laughed.

She realised that they were humming along with her melody, harmonising effortlessly with each note. Her heart skipped a beat as she turned around, for deep down, she suspected she might know who it was.

There stood a striking figure in a smart charcoal suit that made Grace giggle just a little. It was tailored impeccably, the fabric glinting in the sunlight and unravelling the mysteries of simply 'what a suit could be.' It was as if he'd stepped right out of a fashion magazine, exuding an aura of confidence and charm. His dark hair was perfectly tousled, giving him that casual yet refined look that had always captivated Grace.

His voice, rich and velvety, continued the delightful hum, pouring over Grace's own tune. "You've got a lovely voice," Grace admitted, slightly shy but unable to hide the hint of a smile that danced upon her lips. He grinned back, that disarming smile of his that made her forget all about her worries.

Everett!

Grace leaned on her broom as Everett finished serenading her with the sweet strains of one of her favourite songs, 'Ho Hey...' by The Lumineers. His eyes sparkled, a gentle reminder of the kindness in his heart.

"I can't believe you came back," she murmured, half in disbelief, her heart fluttering like a butterfly. She had convinced herself she had blown her chance, that the universe had conspired to keep them apart. And yet, here he was, standing in front of her like a dream turned reality. It felt like a miracle, a twist of fate.

For a moment, silence enveloped them in the lively but empty ice cream shop. Grace and Everett simply looked at each other, and in that gaze, a universe of unsaid words blossomed.

A warmth danced in Grace's chest, urging her to break the silence. She felt a smile trying to escape, hiding just behind the curtain of her lips as if it were a shy child seeking the courage to join in the fun. Everett mirrored her expression, his grin breaking through the earnestness of the moment.

Grace was hiding back a smile. Everett was, too. Then he said, 'Umm, these flowers are to apologize.'

'Apologize?' Grace said.

What does Everett possibly have to apologize for? She thought. 'Yes,' he said, 'I never should have given up on you. You are clearly worth trying and trying and trying again for.'

"I'm sorry if I haven't tried hard enough to get to know you," he admitted, his voice trembling slightly. "I thought you weren't interested in getting to know me."

Grace nodded, casting her gaze on the floor. "I didn't make it easy either. I'm not very confident when it comes to speaking to the opposite sex, especially one I like."

He paused, his expression shifting to one of determination. "I never should have given up on you, Grace. You are clearly worth trying and trying and trying again for."

His words hung in the air, warm and sincere. They struck a chord within Grace, and suddenly, the weight of isolation began to lift. She felt seen, valued, and, most importantly, worth it.

With a shy smile, she replied, "I thought I was the only one feeling this way. It seemed we were both hoping the other would make a move." Their laughter broke the tension, and Grace felt a spark of connection forming between them.

"Let's start again," Everett said, his tone brightening. "Absolutely," Grace enthused, her heart racing with excitement. For the first time in weeks, she felt anticipation blooming within her. This was the beginning of a beautiful friendship… or more, fuelled by clear communication, patience, and, above all, a willingness not to give up.

Everett finally handed Grace the stunning bouquet of flowers he had been holding.

Grace hesitated; this was such a lovely gesture from Everett, but at that moment, it meant so much more to her. Her hands hovered in the air as if she could almost pluck the flowers from his grasp without truly touching them. When was the last time Tim had given her flowers? Had he ever? The memory of Tim's indifference loomed larger than the bouquet in front of her, and she inhaled deeply.

The floral fragrance filled her with emotion, and before she knew it, her carefully kept composure dissolved. Tears sprang to her eyes, unexpected and uncontrollable. She didn't mean to cry; it was just that Everett's kind gesture made her think of a period from her past she had forgotten – one filled with hurt and disappointment, where there were no flowers or kind gestures.

It reminded her of the unearthed emotions she had buried deep. But the more she tried to stop, the more the tears flowed, like a broken dam she had kept hidden for too long.

Everett's expression shifted from pure joy to one of sheer horror, his eyes widening as he searched the ice cream shop for anything that might assist him in the moment. He looked utterly lost.

"Uh, do you need a tissue or something?" he awkwardly asked, his hand scratching the back of his neck. He glanced around as if he expected a magical aide to materialise with a box of tissues.

She didn't really mean to, but once she started, she couldn't stop.

Everett looked horrified. He clearly didn't know what to do. He was overwhelmed, looking around the shop as if something there could help him.

'Did I do something? Say something wrong?' he asked. "I just wanted to apologize for giving up so quickly." He was in total shock at how they had just agreed to start again, seeing Grace turn so suddenly into an emotional wreck in front of him.

Grace couldn't speak. She could only shake her head 'no.' Everett panicked and grabbed a container of white tissues.

"Umm... here?" The words escaped his lips in a half-stutter, his eyes darting around the now dimly lit shop, desperately searching for a semblance of rationality amid Grace's emotional outburst.

Grace couldn't stop the tears. She felt there was something refreshing about shedding tears that were not because of sadness but because of gratitude. The tears were a release she hadn't known she needed. To be treated kindly, to receive such thoughtfulness, and to have someone who cared enough to think about her—it struck a chord deep within her heart.

This thought just made Grace cry even harder.

Chapter 24: Ellie

Ellie was just away from her phone for a minute. Maybe even less than a minute. How long did it take to try on a dress? She paced up and down the changing room, flicking the bright pink dress over her shoulder. After all, it wasn't as if she had been trying to solve the problems of the world? She had simply been examining her reflection in an overly flattering mirror, finding a gorgeous outfit for a date!

"Okay, Ellie," she muttered to herself, "definitely a minute, or maybe two? I mean, how long does it take to try on a dress? As she attempted to strike what she thought could be a model pose — or at least one suited for Instagram.

But the strappy little heels? They did take longer to try on than she expected. Were they truly meant for walking? And then there were the other outfits. The vibrant green A-line skirt, while utterly gorgeous, had put up a fierce fight when trying to get it over her womanly hips.

Yet, when she finally emerged from the changing room, hair slightly askew and a smudge of lipstick on her cheek, reality came crashing in. Ellie's phone had completely blown up. Her eyes scanned over the screen, wide with a mix of disbelief and glee. Ten missed texts? Five missed calls? Catching up was going to need a bigger block of time than just a minute.

Okay, so maybe she was in Shoperapy's dressing room for a little bit longer than she realised.

Then, her heart raced — a message on her blog, too! Her first one! Had she actually stumbled into the world of online fame? "Okay, Ellie, no need to panic — it's just the digital world waiting for your reply," she reassured herself.

But the truth was that she was really excited about dinner with Cameron. Like definitely more excited than she should be, especially considering how recently it was that her heart was shattered into a million pieces.

But in the dressing room, trying on clothes, she'd started to believe again. That love was possible. That she could have it - that the universe hadn't picked her out and said, 'No, no love for you!'

As she slipped into the soft fabric of her stunning pink dress, Ellie couldn't help but picture dinner with Cameron. The way it hugged her curves made her feel like a model from Vogue. Date #1 was only the beginning, but for Ellie, it was the beginning of endless possibilities.

Her mind began to race ahead, weaving its own narrative from the glimmering lights of the restaurant where they would share their first awkward laughs over several clinking wine glasses to Date #2, where she imagined a more intimate setting, perhaps a picnic on the beach.

And then came Date #3. This one was special—the introduction dinner with Cameron's parents. The pressure! "What would she say? Should she mention her love for knitting or her obsession with 90s music?" Every detail crammed into her mind, she laughed, shaking her head at the absurdity of it all.

In her daydreams, Ellie envisioned the proposal—the moment he would kneel and present her with a shiny ring that somehow reflected all her hopes and dreams. "What will I even say?" she questioned. "Yes... but do I need to prepare a speech?!" The pressure of that imaginary moment was almost tangible.

Ellie's imagination soared to the wedding—a fairytale event, complete with flowers, dancing, and perhaps an embarrassing first dance where they would step on each other's toes. Flashes of a future with children popped into her thoughts, too. "A child? Maybe? Why not?" Images of tiny socks and morning chaos filled her mind, followed by another little one—a second child—bringing twice the mess and twice the love.

Finally, she grounded herself in a poignant image: on her deathbed, Cameron leaning in for one last kiss goodbye. Ellie had even teared up at the thought of it – 'Oh, how romantic and lovely it will be!' she whispered, a smile gracing her lips despite the bittersweetness of the moment.

So maybe this was all a good thing, the chaos of her phone. It was like a wake-up call: bad things happen when you get ahead of yourself in love.

She needed to keep a clear head with Cameron. She couldn't keep making the same mistakes!

Ellie looked at Jess's texts first: they're desperate. Asking her where she went. Saying that Adam was there.

There, where? Ellie thinks, confused. Their date wasn't until the next night.

She quickly texted Jess back... "What's happened? Where is Adam?

Next, she checked her comment on her blog, which confused her even more than Jess' texts: 'To the beautiful woman I saw in the café who apparently shops at his store: I meant no harm. I apologize if I offended you. - Levi'

Who is the blogger talking to? Surely not herself.

She scrolled through the latest blog entry on her phone—her brow furrowing deeper with each line. "Who is he talking to? Surely not herself. Could it be Victoria? What shenanigans has she gotten herself into now?"

As she sat on her velvet couch, Ellie couldn't help but laugh at the absurdity. "Maybe Victoria's been up to her usual hijinks and accidentally offended someone. She has a knack for getting herself into trouble and taking no nonsense. I guess that was where Cameron got his troublesome nature from, she mused aloud.

Just as her mind began to spiral deeper into confusion, the bell above the door jingled, pulling her attention back to reality. Ellie was so confused, all twisted around, and then it just got even more confusing!

Through the front door strode Everett—dapper in his grey tailored suit. Chase had done a great job with his makeover. But it wasn't just Everett who walked in. No, he had his arm around Grace, Ellie would have been ecstatic to see this, but Grace was in tears, sniffling and sobbing as Everett looked to her desperately for help.

Ellie's heart sank. What on earth had happened in her absence? Just the other night, they'd all gathered on the beach, celebrating each other, lifting each other up, and moving on.

"What was happening?" Ellie thought, glued to her phone. Jess, Victoria, and Grace—seemed utterly engrossed by their own new dramas. It was as if Ellie had walked in on a soap opera twist.

Jess, her texts were a mix of panic and, I think, joy! Adam showing up early. What was he going to say? What was Jess going to say? Her forehead creased with worry. Would Adam sweep Jess off her feet or let her down gently, devastating her and ending their friendship? If only love came with a user manual and a crystal ball, right?

"Levi? Who even was he?" Was that the married personal trainer Victoria had spoken of? Although I thought his name was Luca. Had Victoria been toying with her heart? Ellie mentally cringed. Not with a married man.

And then there was Grace, her silent sobs punctuating the air as she stood next to Everett, who appeared equally lost. "I just can't stop crying," she sobbed. Seeing her like this was heartbreaking.

"Apparently, love is not on sale today," Ellie quipped to herself, her sense of humour trying to break through the tension. But as Ellie thought of her friends, their flaring frustrations and vulnerable hearts, she couldn't shake a nagging thought: Shoperapy may have been meant to bring love into the world, but first, it had to break down the barriers they'd built around their own hearts. Ellie took a deep breath, her resolve steeling.

What was Ellie supposed to do?

Chapter 25: Ellie

The next morning, sunlight streamed through the large windows of Shoperapy, illuminating the vibrant decor that characterised their favourite haven. Outside, a bright blue sky stretched endlessly, a perfect backdrop for the vibrant flowers blooming in the garden. But inside, the radiant day contrasted sharply with the atmosphere inside.

Three women sat on a selection of vintage couches and chairs; their postures slouched as if the weight of the world rested on their shoulders. Ellie watched them intently, her heart aching for her friends.

Victoria sat with her knees pulled tightly to her chest. The remnants of a sleepless night were evident in the dark circles under her eyes.

Grace lay sprawled on the couch, her hands nervously biting at her nails.

Jess, perched on the pink velvet armchair, could hardly meet their gazes, her fingers twisted in her long, chestnut hair. "After what happened last night, she was embarrassed and had no idea how to make it right with Adam.

Ellie exhaled slowly, absorbing their pain. They had embarked on their love journeys inspired by her encouragement, and now, as she surveyed the scene, it was clear they needed a lifeline—a change of energy, a spark of joy, something to lift their spirits from this low tide of heartache.

"Alright," Ellie declared, mustering her best cheerleader tone, "you can mope until the pancakes arrive, but then no more!" She gestured animatedly as if to chase away the gloom hovering over them.

With a playful flourish, she retrieved a stash of beautifully designed silk pyjamas from her shop—each one unique, just like the women she cared for so deeply. "Here you go," she announced, tossing a pair to each of them. Victoria caught a pair of satin animal print pyjamas, Grace's set was a swirl of vibrant stripes, and Jess's featured soft pastel stars that seemed to twinkle with promise.

"Go on," Ellie encouraged, her eyes sparkling with mischief. "Go put them on!"

The sound of fabric rustling filled the air as they exchanged doubtful glances, but the beginnings of smiles tugged at their lips. They stood slowly, the heaviness of their love lives beginning to lift just a little.

As they walked to the changing rooms, Ellie took a moment to breathe. She could hear light-hearted banter erupting between them as they each tried on their pyjamas, laughter bubbling through the space like a much-needed tonic.

"Wow, these are lovely!" Victoria called out, her voice now tinted with a hint of excitement.

Grace joined in, "I feel like a queen!"

Jess, emerging last and twirling in her pastel pyjamas, grinned widely as she exclaimed, "Who knew pyjamas could be so stylish?"

Ellie couldn't help but smile. This little moment was just the beginning of rekindling their spirits. All she had to do now was sort out her friends heartbreaks, and maybe, just maybe, these women would find their heartbeats dancing again.

Ellie was happy when Chase knocked his knuckle against the glass door of the shop. She hurried over. He had a bag of takeout – pancakes from their favourite local shop.

Chase held up the large bag, and the takeout logo was emblazoned in bright colours. Ellie's eyes widened as she recognised it instantly. "You got the pancakes!" she exclaimed, practically bouncing on her toes. "You didn't forget the extras, did you?" With a flourish, Chase reached into the bag and pulled out two small bottles. One was filled with syrup gleaming like liquid gold, and the other was thick and fluffy whipped cream. "Extra syrup and whipped cream, just like you like it," he replied, grinning with pride.

Chase showed her that he had brought bottles of each. 'How's the mood in there?' he asked.

"You're the best!" Ellie laughed, taking the bottles from him and holding them close as if they were precious jewels. She led him to the back of the shop, where they often snuck away to enjoy their little treats, hidden from the rest of the world.

As they settled down, a comfortable silence fell between them for a moment, only interrupted by the crisp crinkle of the bag as Ellie pulled out the pancakes. "We've been waiting for these," she said, her eyes sparkling with anticipation. "It's been such a strange day, hasn't it?"

"Exactly!" Chase replied, his stomach growling as he reached for his own share. "Pancakes and four gorgeous women—what else do we need?" He took a generous bite, the smooth sweetness of the syrup blending with the fluffy texture of the pancake. A look of bliss came over his face. "Mmm! This is definitely worth the wait."

Ellie giggled, "Right? It's like a little taste of heaven. These should come with an official happiness guarantee or something."

As they finished up their pancakes, the worries of the world outside melted away.

"I just can't believe it," Grace wept. "There's no more tissues."

Ellie turned, her heart tightening at the sight of her friend in distress. As she placed a pancake on a plate, she caught sight of Chase leaning against the backroom counter, arms folded and a cheeky glint in his eye, ready to lighten the mood.

"Good luck, Ellie," he said, a mock of seriousness in his tone. "With all the heartache you've had, you will give the best advice." In response, Ellie rolled her eyes and gave him a light-hearted punch on the shoulder, a playful spark flickering in her gaze. "Thanks for the pancakes, Chase," she chuckled, lightening the atmosphere.

"Just doing my part," he replied, his grin infectious. As he moved towards the door, he added, "Try not to scare them too much with the truth. You know how Grace gets."

With a laugh, Ellie waved him off, a sense of warmth enveloping her heart. He left, and turning back to the table, she took a deep breath, preparing herself for what was about to unfold.

"Alright, ladies," Ellie called out with renewed energy, pouring orange juice into glasses. "Juice, more pancakes, and explanation time." She placed the plates of steaming pancakes on the table, the golden-brown stacks looking incredibly inviting, drizzled with syrup, and sprinkled with berries.

Grace looked up, her eyes still red, but something shifted in her expression—curiosity perhaps? The other women gathered around the table, their expressions a mix of concern and anticipation.

The women go around the room, and all share what happened the night before.

Jess goes first: she was deciding on outfits for her date with Adam the next night when Adam showed up at her door. And what did she do? Did she let him in to talk? Did she get them a bottle of wine as they discussed the possibility of their relationship changing? No. She hid and pretended she wasn't home till Adam left. Even though he knew good and well that she was at home.

Victoria goes next: she wrote a super rude note to the personal trainer, who she thought was cute, who turned out to be married. Only it turns out that she discovered that he wasn't the married personal trainer, but rather his TWIN BROTHER. Victoria was so embarrassed that she didn't have the nerve to reply to the comment. She sat at her computer all night thinking of what to say and ending up saying… nothing. The truth that she doesn't want to admit is that she's actually a little trigger-shy after her divorce – she doesn't yet believe, with her lowered confidence, that someone might be interested in her at this stage of her life. The entire day had been a whirlwind of regret since she sent that note, leaving her suspended in an uncomfortable limbo of shame.

As the evening wore on, Victoria paced her living room, the walls seeming to close in around her. "You should just apologize," she muttered aloud, attempting to convince herself that a simple message might remedy the situation. But every time she contemplated sending a follow-up message, doubt washed over her like a heavy tide. "What if he thinks I'm ridiculous? What if he tells everyone?"

The fact was, Victoria didn't believe she had the confidence needed to connect with someone again, especially a charming personal trainer—even if he wasn't technically married.

Grace is last; she just can't stop crying. Everett was so nice, and it made her think about her relationship with Tim - what was she ever doing with someone like them? Did she not value herself and her happiness? It's all thrown her completely off. And now she might have scared off Everett because she can't. stop. crying!

"Why am I such a mess?" she murmured to herself, but the only answer was the wind whistling through the trees. The thought of Everett—his kind smile and gentle words—made her chest tighten.

His sincerity had caught her off guard. Did he really mean it? She had never experienced such kindness, especially in the midst of her own turmoil. Her mind drifted back to Tim, her boyfriend, who often brushed off her feelings as 'the usual drama.' Did she not value herself enough to seek something better?

For a moment, she wanted to cry even more, to unleash all the confusion and sadness she had bottled up inside. Instead, she forced a shaky smile, wishing she could muster a confident smile.

"I'm such a mess," she confessed. "I didn't want Everett to see me like that. What must he think of me?"

"Everyone has their moments," Ellie reassured her, taking a step forward and now standing directly in front of her. "It doesn't change who you are. Everett will love you just the way you are. You just need to be honest and explain how you're feeling."

'Very good,' Ellie says, nodding. 'Now, let's top off everyone's mimosas, eat more pancakes, and talk it all through…'

Already, the girls felt better being together with their supportive, understanding friends.

The Meadowbank Times

Dear Readers,

Today, I decided to put myself out there, but I was shot down. I wrote a complimentary note to a woman at a café – maybe it's old-fashioned, with all the online dating stuff. But I didn't mean anything bad by it. When he received a strongly worded note back, he went to apologize in the only place he knew she might see it – a website for a clothing store she shopped at, which he knew because her note was on the receipt. But his apology went unanswered. No word at all. So he's moving on, but he's taking a lesson with him: don't put yourself out there, don't try. It's not worth it. Love is dead. No one wants it. If I see a woman wearing clothes from Shoperapy, I'm staying clear!

Chapter 26: Victoria

Victoria nestled comfortably on her terrace, the crisp morning air mingling with the rich aroma of freshly brewed coffee. The sun shimmered over the ocean, creating a tapestry of light that danced across the water's surface. Surrounding her were potted plants, their vibrant greens providing a perfect contrast to the azure backdrop. "This is the life," Victoria sighed contentedly, a hint of a smile curling her lips as she leaned back in her chair. She flicked through the pages of the Sunday paper, her eyes skimming the headlines. Soft notes from her favourite calming music played in the background. "Perhaps a bit of yoga first," she mused aloud, "then a jog on the beach, and maybe later, a healthy dinner—how about grilled salmon?" She could almost taste it.

Yet, as she ventured further into the news, her peaceful morning came to an abrupt halt. "What on earth?" she gasped, nearly dropping her coffee cup. Her heart raced as she read the shocking report. "This can't be real!" she exclaimed, her mind racing to comprehend the implications of what she was reading.

Suddenly distracted by the flavours in her mouth, she had absent-mindedly popped a blackberry in just before reading the astonishing article. The small fruit caught in her throat, prompting a frantic cough.

"Oh no!" she spluttered, choking as the panic set in. Grabbing her cup, she took a swig of coffee, but instead of offering relief, it only sent a searing jolt of heat down her throat.

"Breathe, just breathe!" she urged herself, clutching the arms of her chair. In the chaos, her elbow knocked against the petite side table beside her, sending her portable speaker toppling to the ground, cracking as it hit the floor.

"Not my speaker!" she moaned, eyes darting to the crack, her heart sinking alongside them. "What a mess!" With one final cough, she gasped for air, the choking finally subsiding. "Ahh, there we go," she spluttered, relief washing over her like the gentle waves below.

Shaking her head, she pushed her disheveled hair away from her face, a bemused laugh escaping her lips despite everything. "Well, that's one way to start a Sunday," she chuckled to herself. "I should really watch where I'm going."

After taking a moment to gather her thoughts, she glanced once more at the newspaper, a mixture of intrigue and disbelief swirling within her. "If this is true…" she whispered, the gravity of the news gradually sinking in. Whatever plans she had for the day, it seemed, were about to be altered profoundly.

With a more measured approach, Victoria set her coffee aside, taking a deep breath to steady her racing heart. "Alright, Victoria," she said aloud, a hint of determination seeping into her voice. "Time to face whatever this is." The ether of tranquility had been replaced by a wave of adrenaline, and while her heart still felt unsettled, curiosity propelled her to explore the intrigue of her Sunday newspaper.

Victoria was casually leafing through the Sunday paper over a cup of coffee on her terrace overlooking the ocean. She had on some nice, calming music. She had a relaxing, stress-free day planned ahead of her - maybe some yoga, maybe a little jog or swim, and maybe a nice, healthy dinner for herself later on.

But suddenly, she was so surprised by what she read that she started to choke on a blackberry. Drinking to clear her throat only makes it worse as the hot coffee scalds her. She knocks over the little side table where her stereo was, breaking her stereo. Finally, she can breathe.

But she is the furthest thing in the world, from relaxed to stress-free. How did the morning turn from that to nearly dying! Victoria glanced again at what had startled her so terribly in the newspaper. Her cheeks get red as she skims it over… oh, no, she thinks, this is not good. Not good at all.

As she gets to the end, she realizes this isn't just a problem for her. It's a problem for Shoperapy… It's a problem for Ellie.

"Okay, let's see…" she muttered to herself, searching frantically for her white blouse. "I just need to look decent. Not too fancy, but not too casual either." The butterflies in her stomach fluttered violently, reminding her of the importance of this day.

Finally, Victoria found the blouse, crinkled but acceptable, and pulled it over her head. She glanced at herself in the mirror, the reflection showing a face that was still somewhat unsure.

"Not bad, Vic," she encouraged, forcing a smile that didn't quite reach her eyes. "Just make sure you're confident."

In the middle of her frantic routine, she remembered she could use something to cover up. She dashed back into her room and grabbed a lilac shrug. "This should do the trick," she said quietly, her voice almost lost amidst the storm of thoughts swirling in her mind.

With her appearance somewhat in order, she raced out of the house, her foot tapping anxiously against the pavement as she walked. Victoria navigated through the bustling streets of town, her mind racing just as fast as her feet.

"Breathe, just breathe," she whispered, attempting to calm herself. "It's just Ellie. You've been friends too long for her to flip out."

But images of their past conversations crept in like shadows, following her every step. What would she say? How could she bring up the subject? As the buildings whizzed by, she tried to compose her thoughts, each attempt at clarity only clouded by self-doubt.

"I'll just start with something light. Maybe a joke?" she suggested out loud, the scariness of the situation creeping in like a winter chill. "Or perhaps, 'How about we chat over coffee? It's always good to catch up!'"

Victoria shook her head at herself, laughing nervously. "Great, Vic. Very casual. What if she doesn't react well? What if she gets upset, and I don't know how to respond?" Her brow furrowed in concentration as she crossed yet another busy intersection.

At last, she arrived at Shoperapy, the little café that had become their unofficial meeting ground. Taking a deep breath, she reminded herself of the warmth and understanding Ellie had always shown her, how they'd navigated their challenges together.

"Remember the last time we were here?" she thought, grinning slightly at the memory of sharing cupcakes and giggles. "It can't go wrong. You've got this."

Once inside, Victoria spotted Ellie sitting at their usual table, a steaming cup of tea before her. Ellie looked up, her eyes sparkling with delight as she waved. "Victoria! I'm so glad you made it! I was beginning to think I'd have to drink this all on my own."

"You know I can never let that happen," Victoria replied, forcing casualness into her tone as she slid into the chair opposite Ellie.

"But not to be rude, what's the deal with the fancy tea today?"

Ellie grinned but paused, sensing the underlying tension. "You seemed a bit rushed getting here... everything alright?"

Victoria's heart raced again, her earlier bravado wavering. "Well, actually... there's something I need to talk to you about." She took a deep breath, feeling weighty at the moment. "I've been working on... well, you know, feeling better about myself."

Ellie leaned in, concern etching across her face. "Of course. I'm here for you, whatever it is."

As the words hung in the air, the café buzzed around them, but all that mattered was the gentle understanding radiating from Ellie, a reminder that love and support were never far away.

Victoria hurried to get ready and get out of the house. Still, she darted back inside to grab a shrug to cover up. She'd made a lot of progress with the body self-confidence issues, but she was still not there all the way.

She hurried across town to Shoperapy. She was going to break it to Ellie gently. She'd find the right words, so the blow wasn't too bad. She was practising on the way over.

Victoria was super apologetic, but Ellie reassured her that it was fine.

The bell jingled softly as Victoria stepped into the quaint little shop nestled between the bustling café and a tiny bookshop, where the scent of freshly brewed coffee mingled with the sweet aroma of pastries. She paused, letting her eyes adjust to the warm, inviting glow of the overhead lights. It was a charming haven; shelves lined with vibrant handcrafted goods, delicate ceramics, and beads that sparkled as if to compete with the early afternoon sun cascading through the window.

Ellie was busy arranging the latest batch of handmade candles on a display table, a slight frown creasing on her forehead. Victoria could tell that her friend was feeling the strain of the past few weeks. "Hey, Ellie," she called out, forcing a bright smile despite the clouds of concern hanging over her.

Ellie turned, a look of relief washing over her features. "Oh, Victoria! I'm so glad you're here," she replied, her voice warm and bright but with an undertone of weariness. "I thought I might have to tackle another slow afternoon all on my own."

Grace and Jess walked in, too. They had also read the editorial and came right away.

The issue is Levi's 'anonymous' opinion piece in the newspaper. Victoria knew that it was all her fault. She should have reached out to Levi, apologized, and explained. She waited too late... and now this.

She knew how hard it had been for Ellie to get customers into the shop - as a freelance editor, she knew that starting any business was an uphill battle.

The last thing in the world she needed right now was bad press of any kind.

"I know how hard it's been for you to get customers into the shop," Victoria said, stepping closer. As a freelance editor, she understood the daunting challenge of starting a business. "It's an uphill battle, isn't it?"

Ellie nodded, her shoulders slumping momentarily. "It really is," she sighed, brushing a strand of hair behind her ear. "The last thing in the world I need right now is bad press of any kind."

With an apologetic tone, Victoria pressed her lips together. "I didn't mean for any of that to happen, Ellie. I truly thought my blog would bring more attention to your shop, not drive customers away."

Ellie straightened suddenly, her usual chipper demeanour returning. "Oh, Vic, stop that! Look, I have all these brilliant women here to help," she said, spreading her arms wide to encompass Jess and Grace, who had entered the shop with their own bags filled with supplies. "We're going to find a solution to this, I know it!"

Jess chimed in, a flicker of determination in her eyes. "Exactly, there's nothing we can't solve together! If we need to launch a proper campaign or set up some fun events, I'm in!"

Grace nodded fervently, her curls bouncing with enthusiasm. "And we could offer some promotional discounts! Encourage customers to try different products! It could really help your visibility."

Victoria felt a swell of admiration for the way they banded together, a circle of support in a sea of uncertainties. But amidst the encouragement, Ellie paused, suddenly realising the more immediate concern. "You know what?" she said, putting her hands on her hips, a playful grin breaking through. "The most important thing we need to decide now is what to order for lunch. I have a craving for those cheese pastries from that little bakery down the road."

"And whether we should pair it with a red or a white!" Jess added with a laugh.

Ellie threw her head back and let out a light-hearted laugh, the lift in her spirits palpable. "Just remember, a good wine can fix everything!"

"Yes, it absolutely can!" Grace agreed, her eyes twinkling with mischief.

As they all began to chatter excitedly about lunch choices, with a few friendly jabs at each other's tastes, Victoria felt a weight lifting from her chest. Here in this little shop, surrounded by warmth, laughter, and friendship, she realised that they would find their way through all challenges together.

And as the afternoon wore on, so did their plans.

Sweet and positive as always, Ellie says, 'Look, I have all these brilliant women here to help. We're going to find a solution to this. I know it!'

Jess and Grace agree - there's nothing they can't solve together.

Ellie said that the most important thing to decide now was what to order for lunch. And whether a red or a white goes better.

Victoria hugged Ellie. She was so happy to have found such a great friend. She thought Ellie was going to be so mad.

Dear Readers,

Sometimes, people go all out there on a limb. Sometimes, there are innocent mistakes for which the author is sorry, but that doesn't mean she wouldn't say yes should she get the chance a second time... Sometimes, people have emotional baggage and are afraid of putting themselves out there. Sometimes, people just need more time to respond to apologies written on an online blog. And sometimes people who like someone they meet in public just need to be a little more patient.   Anonymous

Chapter 27: Grace

Grace almost told Ellie the truth that night when she was rescued from her table and dragged along to Shoperapy for a night of shopping - she felt bad that Ellie was being so nice under false assumptions.

And she felt even worse when she found out how fiercely Ellie defended her against Cameron, whose fault it wasn't.

Grace sat beside her cluttered table, glancing anxiously at her phone for the fourth time in two minutes. She should have been enjoying her evening, surrounded by the stylish racks of Shoperapy, yet the weight of her secret pinned her to the seat like a lead blanket. Ellie was bustling around her, admiring a deep blue dress that swayed delicately as she twirled.

"Grace, come on! You've got to try this on!" Ellie exclaimed, her eyes sparkling with excitement and her voice bubbling with uncontainable cheer.

With a hesitant sigh, Grace allowed Ellie to drag her from her seat. "I just... I'm not really in the mood, Ellie," she mumbled quietly, her eyes darting to the ground.

"But you've been doing that too much lately!" Ellie said, a tinge of concern creeping into her voice. "You shouldn't hide away from the world. You deserve to have fun, especially tonight."

Grace felt a pang of guilt. Ellie didn't know the truth, and she didn't know what was really happening. "I feel like I'm lying to you," she whispered, her voice barely audible.

Ellie stopped and turned to her, brow furrowed. "You're not lying!

You're just... avoiding something, aren't you?"

The truth was, Grace was scared. She wanted to scream everything out, to tell Ellie that she didn't want to date Cameron and that she arrived early so she could say he stood her up, when he didn't. That she was still in love with Tim and truly believed he would come back for her.

They wandered deeper into the shop, Ellie chatting away, pointing out outfits, always with a genuine enthusiasm that Grace would normally find infectious. But tonight, every word felt like another weight upon her conscience. As Ellie enthused over a pair of heels, Grace felt her heart shatter a little more. She shouldn't be here, pretending everything was fine.

"Look at these!" Ellie exclaimed, holding up a pair of bright pink heels, her excitement palpable. "You would totally rock these, Grace! They'd bring out the colour in your eyes!"

"Ellie, I—" Grace tried to interject, her words tumbling like stones in her throat. But the words never made it out. Instead, Ellie continued to gush about how fabulous they would look at the next party, blissfully unaware of the turmoil raging inside Grace.

Later, as they strolled out of the shop, Ellie wrapped an arm around Grace's shoulders. "You know, you can tell me anything, right? I'd defend you to the ends of the Earth," Ellie said softly, her warmth radiating reassurance.

At that moment, Grace almost confessed her fears. Almost. "I know, Ellie. And I'll tell you soon, I promise," she replied, her heart heavy with remorse yet warm with gratitude, the battle within her raging on.

But she hadn't been brave enough - wasn't that always Grace's problem? Too shy. Too timid. Too quiet. Too afraid.

The night Grace pulled her trick on Cameron, she didn't have any reservations - she wasn't interested in Cameron. Didn't know him, except that her friends said he was hot. She wasn't invested at all.

But this time, on her way (way too early!) for a date with Everett, she was hesitant - was she throwing away a good thing because she was afraid?

Grace was still undecided about what she would do when she arrived at the restaurant, where she insisted that she make the reservation. What would she do? Would she wait? Or would she go before he arrives like she did with Cameron?

But to Grace's surprise, Everett was already there!

The evening air was filled with the sweet scent of summer as Grace entered the restaurant, the waitress welcoming her like an old friend. Her palms felt clammy, and she could sense the flutter of her heartbeat as she scanned the room, looking for Everett. There he was, sitting at a small table by the window, his gaze fixed on the flowers in front of him. A quaint bouquet of daisies and violets, their vibrant colours contrasting sharply with the stark white tablecloth.

Taking a deep breath, she approached him, each step feeling like a mile. "Hey, sorry I'm late!" she said, forcing a smile. Everett looked up, his blue eyes wide with a mixture of surprise and delight.

"Grace!" he exclaimed, his voice warm and inviting. "I'm so glad you could make it."

He was surprised to see her, too, and they both laughed.

Everett explained that he was so nervous and excited that he wanted to be early. He didn't plan to be that early, but before he knew it, he was out his front door and on his way.

He stood up hurriedly, perhaps too hastily, and in his fluster, he knocked over a glass of water. It toppled off the table, cascading towards the floor and creating a small puddle.

"Oh no!" Grace laughed as she instinctively reached for a napkin, trying to help. "You're a bit clumsy, aren't you?"

Everett chuckled, embarrassment creeping onto his cheeks. "Yeah, I guess I am. I just wanted everything to be perfect for you." He leaned forward, setting the bouquet down carefully in front of her. "These are for you."

Grace's heart swelled. She took them from Everett, inhaling their fresh fragrance. "They're lovely, thank you!" She felt a flicker of confidence; maybe this date could turn out better than she expected.

"You look beautiful, by the way," he added, his gaze lingering on her floral dress.

"Really?" Grace felt her cheeks warm. She twirled slightly, allowing the hem of her dress to float around her. "I wasn't sure about it. I thought it might be too much."

"No," he assured her, his smile genuine. "It's perfect." He stood up straight and held out her chair for her, his gesture smooth and courteous. "Please, have a seat."

He had flowers for her; he complimented her dress and pulled out her chair for her - the perfect gentleman, although he did knock over a glass of water on the table, giving her the flowers. Grace, who had been so unsure, was sure now. She decided to stay and give it a shot - a real shot.

Grace realised what a great match for her Everett was: he wasn't super brave either. He was shy, just like her. But it didn't matter. He liked her and wanted her to be happy, and that was what mattered to Grace the most.

As she settled into her chair, Grace couldn't help but notice how naturally he navigated his nervousness. "You know," she said, attempting to steer the conversation, "I've always thought that shyness could be quite endearing. It means you care."

Everett looked thoughtful, his brow furrowing slightly. "I do care. But sometimes I feel like I'm a bit too shy."

"Me too," Grace replied, her voice softening. "I've always found it difficult to open up, especially on first dates, but there's something about being here with you that feels... right."

The air between them shifted, tension replaced by understanding. Everett leaned in a little closer, his expression earnest. "I've been nervous the whole time leading up to this"

"Really? I thought you seemed so composed," Grace teased, her laughter light.

"Quite the act, I assure you," he replied with a sheepish grin. They both shared a moment of silence, each caught in the serenity of this unexpected connection. Grace's heart raced, the uncertainty in her mind replaced by clarity. She wanted to stay and give this a real shot — a true chance at something more.

As the evening wore on, they talked and laughed, discovering common interests and dreams for the future. Everett, she realised, wasn't super brave either; he was shy, just like her. Yet, in that shared vulnerability, Grace understood that love was not about grand gestures or loud proclamations. Love, she thought, was simply wanting the other person to be happy, knowing that both could be brave together, and that maybe, just maybe, this was the beginning of something beautiful.

Grace was having a lovely time when her phone buzzed. She checked it beneath the table.

She couldn't believe it. It was Tim calling!

This was what she had been hoping for all along! The one thing she'd prayed for, wished upon stars for, dreamed of. It was what was once her happily ever after.

But it wasn't even a hard decision.

Grace hit the ignore button and focused her attention back on Everett.

Chapter 28: Jess

Jess rhythmically drummed her thumbs on the steering wheel, the sound creating a fidgety hum in the otherwise nearly silent car. Ahead of her was a seemingly endless stretch of red brake lights, resembling the world's longest uninvited queue. Bumper to bumper, it felt as if the city had conspired to sabotage her evening with Adam, the man she had eagerly anticipated meeting all week. The vibrant remnants from the summer market lined the road, yet all Jess could focus on was time slipping away, each tick of the clock on her dashboard whispering sweetly of her impending tardiness. With her heels discarded in the passenger seat, she felt the coolness of the car's floor beneath her bare feet and briefly contemplated how utterly ridiculous she must look—barefoot and panicking amid the city traffic.

A quick glance at the time set her heart racing. She was on the verge of being late—worse than late, in fact. Every nerve in her body screamed at her as the dreadful reality sank in: she might be stuck in this gridlock for the entire evening. What a disaster... again. The mere thought of it made her groan audibly, a sound barely heard over the droning engine. Anxiety bubbled up inside her, suffocating her rational thoughts like a thick fog rolling into the city.

Had she purposefully left later than she ought to have? A question that nagged at her mind, refusing to dissipate. She was well familiar with the chaos of city streets—this was her daily commute, after all. Yet here she was, ensnared, fully aware of how unpredictable rush hour could be. Why hadn't she set off earlier?

As she wrestled with this internal tempest, her thoughts drifted to the evening's myriad misfortunes. It wasn't her fault that she had sneezed precisely at the moment she was applying her mascara, was it? That was simply the capricious will of nature; no one could fault her for that. However, the aftermath— a frantic effort to tidy up her face and reapply her foundation and concealer—had cost her at least an extra ten minutes.

Moreover, who could have predicted that her trusty scissors would go missing at such a critical juncture? She always placed them in the same drawer; they were almost a security blanket for her outfits, yet they had vanished just when she needed them most. Classic luck, Jess thought dryly.

She shook her head in frustration. Every element of her outfit had been meticulously planned with Ellie over coffee, from the perfect dress down to those vibrant red heels. Yet they hadn't scrutinised her purse. Everyone knew that a purse could make or break an outfit. When a girl invested so much effort, it was only natural for a guy to remember every detail, right down to the bag she carried. Right?... Right?

As if on cue, the traffic began to inch forward, offering her a flimsy glimmer of hope. But before long, that hope was snatched away as the vehicle in front lurched forward slightly, only to come to a sudden halt. Jess let out an exasperated huff; the evening seemed intent on teasing her mercilessly.

Within her mind, she conjured a vision of how splendid the evening with Adam could unfold—laughter over cocktails, chemistry simmering to life as they reminisced about shared memories. However, the image quickly warped into a montage of potential disasters: arriving late, fumbling for excuses, and the awkward silences that might stretch between them as he wondered if she was perhaps too scatterbrained for someone like him.

Just then, the radio crackled to life, pulling Jess's thoughts back to the present. A familiar tune flooded the car's interior, and for a fleeting moment, her anxiety retreated in the face of nostalgia. She tapped her fingers against the steering wheel in time for the beat, a small smile creeping onto her face as she hummed along. Perhaps this was a reminder to lighten up and embrace the situation, even if it was not what she had envisioned. Who knew? A bit of humour at her expense could render the evening all the more memorable.

Did she subconsciously do it on purpose? The thought was unsettling. To be late on purpose? To avoid Adam and what he might say…? Surely not. She shook her head vehemently, wishing the notion would dissipate like the fog around her.

"Maybe I should call him?" she muttered to herself, glancing at the clock that seemed to mock her with its relentless ticking. Five more minutes ticked away, the neon lights of the cafe flickering invitingly in the distance but feeling impossibly far. After another internal battle, she reached for her phone, fingertips trembling slightly as she dialed.

"Hey, it's, uh, Jess," she said when Adam picked up, her voice unsteady despite the casual tone she tried to adopt. "Traffic is horrible, like, seriously bad. I'm going to be really, really late." "Don't worry about it," Adam responded, his voice warm and reassuring. "It's fine. I'll wait. I really want to see you."

What he said was exactly what Jess should want to hear, yet a wave of discomfort washed over her. She squirmed in her chair, the leather creaking in protest. A strange reluctance blossomed within her, an urge to retreat back into the safety of uncertainty. "No," she blurted out, heart racing. "No, we should probably just reschedule." The words felt both liberating and suffocating as they escaped her lips.

Adam's silence on the other end of the line only amplified her anxiety. The air felt thick with unspoken questions, and Jess could almost hear his thoughts racing. She imagined him biting his lip, trying to gauge her mood, assessing what was behind her decision.

Did he suspect the truth? That she was afraid, not of him but of what it meant to step out from her carefully built walls? "Jess," he finally said, cautious now, "Are you sure? I mean, I can just grab a coffee, and you can—"

"No, Adam! I really think it's best," she interrupted, the urgency bubbling over. Yet, even as she spoke, she felt a pang of regret creeping in. Perhaps it was the rain tapping against her windshield, each droplet echoing her inner turmoil.

"Alright," he said slowly, "If that's what you want, I'll just head home."

Jess rested her head against the steering wheel, the weight of disappointment heavy on her shoulders. She stared at the cafe, the warm glow beckoning like a beacon. If only she could muster the courage to walk through those doors.

Instead, she sat, lost in thought. Another part of her wanted to go. To see him. To feel that electric connection they shared.

But another part screamed at her to stay put, to remain cloaked in the comfort of her fears.

Jess chuckled to herself in ironic disbelief. What a predicament. All she had wanted was a simple date with Adam, yet she turned it into this complicated mess. "Just a little coffee," she whispered, her voice laced with self-mockery.

Yet, here she was, avoiding it all, wondering if her heart was truly ready to take such a leap. Maybe next time... but right now, she needed to breathe, caught in a battle of wants and worries, her heart tethered between fear and affection.

"Are you sure we should just go home, Jess? We could still meet at McDonalds, at a gas station, at the side of the road!" Adam said, trying one more time to convince Jess to keep going.

But Jess was now even more convinced they'd never find a place with an open table at this hour - "impossible!"

Jess got more and more desperate.

'Don't be silly,' she said. 'We'll do this another time. I'm heading home. I will see you at work.'

Jess hung up and then got off the highway at the nearest exit. As she drove towards home, she realised this was all a mistake.

She never should have thought she could be more than just friends with Adam.

Now, she had ruined everything. She could never face him again.

Jess was going to have to switch jobs. Maybe leave the city…

Jess's thoughts spiraled out of control from the fear of what Adam was going to say to her.

Chapter 29: Victoria

The sauna was dimly lit, an embodiment of Finnish design, adorned entirely in light wood with benches meticulously arranged around a large, gleaming heater. Following an intense workout with Cameron, Victoria often found solace in her favourite corner—the one closest to the heat. It enveloped her like a cocoon, wrapping her in warmth as she settled in, allowing the tension in her muscles to dissolve.

This sauna served as her sanctuary, the sole place within the gym—and indeed, the only venue outside her own home— where she felt entirely at ease, revealing her arms. Clad in her sports bra, the soft glow of the sauna light enhanced the shimmer of her skin, glistening with a fine sheen of sweat. Leaning her head back against the wall, Victoria closed her eyes, surrendering to the peaceful quiet that enveloped her. Here, she didn't need to feign bravery or assume any façade. This space offered not merely relaxation, but a moment of pure bliss where she could simply exist.

Of course, her 'revenge body'—a term she laughed over with friends—fuelled her obsession with the gym. The results were gratifying, yet it was the sauna that truly worked its magic on her spirit. With each drop of sweat, she felt lighter, both physically and emotionally, as if the humid air was cleansing away her worries, leaving her with clarity.

Suddenly, the door of the sauna creaked open, and ordinarily, she would not have bothered to open her eyes; the dimness acted like a veil, shielding her from the external world. Furthermore, it was far too hot to concern herself with what someone else might think of her. The notion of judgement could crinkle her tranquility, and she preferred not to entertain it for even a moment. Instead, she absorbed the warmth, relishing this stolen time that was entirely hers—unbothered and unapologetic.

However, a faint laugh pierced the tranquility, and a smile tugged at the corners of her mouth. "Definitely not my best look," she mused, envisioning the newcomer's surprised expression as they glanced at her with a mix of intrigue and bemusement. Uncertain of their identity, she opted to keep her eyes firmly shut and embrace the absurdity—a beauty in vulnerability, she thought—a personal joke within the steaming silence.

It was the only time she felt this way, and she had no intention of jeopardising that sensation by looking to see if someone was observing her.

Yet, a small noise—something akin to a sigh, a scoff, or a chuckle—compelled her to open her eyes this time.

Victoria shifted on the wooden bench, acutely aware of the awkward silence that loomed between them. She had longed for solitude, yet fate seemed to possess a sense of humour. With every teasing glance from Luca, her heart flickered between annoyance and amusement. His persistent presence felt even more pronounced, particularly with the gleaming wedding ring that reproached her under the faint glow of the sauna light.

After a moment of contemplating her response, Victoria raised her gaze, a smirk forming as she finally spoke. "Could you please inform your brother that he's being ridiculous?" she said, her tone infused with mischief that danced through the steam. Luca appeared genuinely puzzled for a heartbeat, his brow furrowing as he attempted to process her words.

"My brother?" he repeated incredulously, eyes widened as though she had proposed he swim in a pool of ice rather than convey his brother's folly.

"Yes, your brother," she retorted, her laughter bubbling like the steam enveloping them. "Honestly, I fail to understand what he was thinking, believing that sending me flowers constituted a good idea! Does he think a bouquet can substitute for common sense?"

Luca chuckled, finally alleviating the tension. "I do believe it was an exceptionally poor choice on his part," he replied, amusement evident on his face. "But just to clarify, I reckon flowers were a lovely notion... albeit misplaced."

Victoria leaned back against the wall, the heat now feeling more welcoming as humour interspersed with the atmosphere. "He must have taken more than a few knocks to the head."

Luca arched an eyebrow, unable to resist the playful banter. "Well, if he has, perhaps it's time I kept a closer watch on him." "It was an honest mistake," Victoria insisted, her voice a blend of exasperation and sincerity. "And I've apologised." She observed Luca's brow furrowing, his expression a puzzle she struggled to decipher.

Luca nodded, yet his silence felt like a heavy burden, hanging between them like a dense fog. There was something in his eyes that hinted at disappointment, yet he kept it to himself. Victoria drummed her fingers against the bench, convinced there was little more to address. After all, she had delivered her verdict, signed and sealed, but not entirely communicated. She attempted to close her eyes once more, working to refocus on relaxation amid the chaos of the evening, yet it felt as if an itch had taken residence beneath her skin, an obstinate annoyance she couldn't ignore.

She huffed in irritation, the sound escaping her lips unbidden. "Honestly, it was just ketchup on my new blouse! It's not like I set fire to your favourite trainers." A faint grin threatened to emerge, revealing the absurdity of the situation. Yet, the weight of unexpressed feelings lingered in the air.

Victoria tilted her head, half in earnest but mostly teasing, hopeful for a spark of humour and camaraderie.

"Do you not agree he's being ridiculous?" Victoria queried. "Your brother?"

Luca's grin widened.

"Why are you grinning like that?" Victoria asked, her eyebrows arching in confusion. The corners of Luca's mouth betrayed him, curling upwards as if he knew a secret she did not. Her frustration escalated to an impending boil. She folded her arms across her chest, attempting to contain the simmering heat of her irritation. "Honestly, Luca, this isn't a game. I've outgrown games."

"Perhaps I merely find it amusing," he teased, his grin deepening as he gauged her reaction.

Victoria rolled her eyes, exuding the dramatic flair of a Shakespearean actress. "You think this is humorous?" she exclaimed. "I'm far beyond wanting riddles and witty banter. The truth is, I'm primarily too old to play games in love. I desire straightforwardness and honesty, period. Look at us! We're not children any longer!"

For a fleeting moment, silence draped over them like a thick fog, and she could nearly hear the echoes of all the 'what-ifs' suspended in the air. The laughter that once permeated their conversations felt like a distant memory, glimmering like sunlight on water but now veiled in uncertainty's gloom.

"Okay, I hear you," Luca finally replied, his grin fading. "However, it's challenging to be 'straightforward' when attempting to discern what the other person genuinely desires."

Victoria sighed, the tension easing slightly. "All I wish for is straightforward honesty."

Luca fell silent for a moment. Victoria's breath came in heavy gasps, her heart racing as though she had just completed a marathon. She still felt the adrenaline surging through her veins. How could he simply stand there, grinning as if he had won some prize? It infuriated her.

"Why are you smiling like that?" she snapped, her frustration bubbling to the surface like an overboiling pot. Luca leaned back against the wall, his smile widening, as though he had crafted the world's best joke.

"Because I said I told you so!" he replied with an insufferably carefree tone that ignited her desire to strangle him.

Victoria rolled her eyes, crossing her arms tightly over her chest, striving to suppress her irritation. "Honestly, I don't find your teasing amusing right now."

"Oh, come on! You must admit, you needed to brush up on your technique," he beamed, his voice laden with that infuriating light-heartedness.

Her face flushed, and momentarily, she battled the urge to chuckle despite the irritation. How could he manage to inject humour into any situation? Just as she was about to berate him, he poked her lightly in the ribs, and she erupted into laughter, shaking her head. "You're impossible, Luca!"

Then, laughing, he quipped, "Do you think Luca and I need to start wearing name tags?"

Chapter 30: Ellie

Ellie could hardly comprehend the reality of the situation— her date with Cameron was actually happening. If someone had asked her on the night of her Grand Opening after he had first stormed into Shoperapy whether it was more likely for her to end up on a date with him or wanted for his murder, it would not have been a difficult bet to make. Yet, astonishingly, there she was.

The restaurant he had chosen epitomised her tastes: a charming bistro nestled on a cobbled street, softly illuminated by fairy lights that twinkled like stars confined in glass jars. Upon stepping inside, Ellie was embraced by the aroma of fresh herbs and sizzling garlic. The intimate atmosphere, punctuated by a gentle hum of conversation and the occasional outburst of laughter, formed a symphony of joy that made her heart flutter.

Soft jazz filled the air, harmonising with the clinking of cutlery and the delicate rustle of napkins being arranged on tables. The walls were adorned with whimsical art pieces, including a painting of a feline in a bowler hat hovering above a selection of vintage whisky bottles, which added an eccentric charm that Ellie found delightful.

Things were off to a good start: Cameron had done good.

Ellie had only to think the thought, and there he was, spotting her across the room at the exact moment that she spotted him. He wore a crooked smile that sent her stomach tumbling. At that moment, enveloped by the restaurant's enchantment, a glimmer of hope ignited within her—perhaps they could do more than snap at each other's throats after all. Fighters became lovers sometimes, didn't they?

Everything seemed perfect! Dressed in a remarkably handsome suit—an ensemble she might have considered for her shop, should she ever expand into menswear – Cameron cut a dapper figure as he pulled out her chair for her. He'd even brought her a charming bouquet of flowers. The weather was idyllic—a warm evening, kissed by a gentle breeze. A glorious sunset yielded to twinkling stars in the deepening sky.

Ellie could scarcely find a single fault in the night thus far. Seated at a small, intimate table in the restaurant, the waiter, glancing over with a knowing smile, assumed them to be a couple deeply in love. A gentle chuckle escaped her lips.

"Everyone thinks we're a match made in heaven," she teased, glancing around the restaurant.

Cameron's grin widened, his eyes glistening with mischief. "Well, we certainly weren't made in heaven," he replied. "But maybe we can end up there."

Ellie smiled. She hardly knew what to say when Cameron was being nice to her. If he wanted to argue about just who caused their less-than-heavenly start, she'd be game. It made her excited, the thought of locking her horns with his. But they were in a nice restaurant, having a nice dinner, and it seemed that the boxing gloves had to stay hung up in the closet.

After a few moments of peaceful silence, Cameron asked her politely how the shop was doing.

Ellie wrapped her hands around a steaming cup of tea, which the waiter had just dropped off. A light sigh escaped her.

"It's a bit slow, to be honest," she said. "I want to find a way to bring in new customers, but I'm uncertain how."

"How about putting up some vibrant photos on the walls?" he suggested enthusiastically. "Capture happy customers enjoying their time? It will create a warm atmosphere! When you have the photos, I could help you hang them up."

Ellie's eyes narrowed, and a grin played at her lips. "That sounds like a trap," she said.

Cameron laughed. "I swear it's not."

Ellie watched him carefully.

"You think I don't have happy customers to take pictures of because I'm too stubborn," she said.

"I know you have happy customers," Cameron said.

Drumming her fingers, she said, "You plan to drive away business with the noise of the hammer."

"I'll do it after closing time," he said. "You—"

Cameron reached across the table and took Ellie's. His touch was warm like the sun on a perfectly clear day. No storm clouds in sight.

"No tricks, no plans, no secret motives," he said. "We're turning a page, Ellie. No more fighting. No more backstabbing."

Ellie hesitated a moment more. Cameron held up his pinkie finger. Ellie wrapped hers around his.

"Alright then," Ellie said, nodding. "No more fighting. No more backstabbing."

So it was a truce, like Cameron had said, a blank page. A fresh start. Normal love. Sweet love. Gentle love. Ellie could get on board with that... couldn't she?

For the whole rest of the evening, their conversation went in an easy back-and-forth. It was all ideal for a first date with the immediate promise of a second: a little echo of flirtation, questions that felt genuine, and delightful bits of laughter.

After the pinkie promise, Ellie shed the snarky sass of their initial interactions. She hardly teased him at all. Instead, she embodied the role of a pleasant lady, her hands folded neatly in her lap—no wagging fingers tonight! With delicate movements, she dabbed her napkin against the corners of her lips, never even considering hurling it in Cameron's direction and storming out. They shared a dessert, each insisting the other should take the last bite of cake, refusing to be the one to claim it if the other desired it. In the end, the waiter took the plate with the last bite untouched. Ellie wanted to say it was ridiculous; Cameron should have taken it. In fact, she very much wanted to argue about it. But Cameron smiled with tightly pressed lips, so she did the same. Peace.

How... nice.

They settled the bill as it should have been settled, with Cameron adamantly insisting on paying and Ellie pretending dismay for a moment or two before relenting. Cameron stood to assist her back into her jacket. As they left the restaurant, they hailed a cab ("I'm not allowing you to take the bus, not on my watch."), offering to cover the fare back home. Check, check, and check. He'd done everything right. The perfect date.

The perfect gentleman.

As they waited at the curb for the cab, Ellie noticed how the night air was neither hot nor cold, the perfect kiss of the softest breeze. The perfect song for a romantic end to a romantic evening started playing from the restaurant's outdoor speakers. They were perfectly alone. Her stomach even had the perfect amount of butterflies as Cameron scratched nervously at the back of his neck and glanced down at her before looking quickly away. She was just the perfect amount of excitement.

Cameron picked the perfect moment to lean in – just as she tucked her hair shyly behind her ear. Closing her eyes involuntarily, Ellie surrendered to the moment. Love's true kiss. The magic of something is beginning. The fragile touch builds a strong foundation. The hope of forever in just a few precious seconds. Every element of the night had synchronised, starry sky, gentle breeze, and laughter that waltzed in the moonlight. This was love, and it felt undeniably right.

Right?

Cameron pulled away and cleared his throat. "Um…"

Ellie forced a smile. "That was really…"

Cameron shuffled his feet. She reached for the right words. They spoke over each other in a tumble of 'um's' and 'well's'. Both stopped. Neither started again. Ellie could suddenly hear the rough scratch of teenager's skateboards. The breeze pushed her hair into her lip gloss.

Breathing deeply, Cameron tried again. "That wasn't…"

He looked down at her. Ellie sighed next. She nodded. "Yeah, that wasn't great."

When Cameron kissed her, Ellie's heart had fluttered the way it should have fluttered. Her eyes closed without her even telling them. Everything had been the way it should have been. And yet…

Cameron tugged at his earlobe nervously. "There was no…"

"Spark," Ellie replied.

"I was going to say fire." Ellie crossed her arms.

"Spark' is a better way to put it, though," she said, turning back towards him. "A spark is the beginning of something. A fire, well, that's not the right way to put it at all. Maybe you could say 'fire' for a kiss after a long time away from each other or during a passionate makeup after a terrible fight."

Cameron turned towards Ellie as well. They each had their arms crossed over their chests. Each were breathing more heavily than they had the entire night. There was more colour in their cheeks, too.

"But a spark isn't guaranteed to catch," Cameron argued. "A spark may just go out right on the spot. A fire, now that's heat, that's a promise, that's something."

Ellie was about to argue back, but instead just stood there beneath all those stars and grinned. After a moment, she shook her head.

"Such a shame," she said. "What?" Cameron asked.

"Can I be honest with you for a second?" Ellie asked. "That's never stopped you before," Cameron said wryly.

Ellie bit her lip, hesitant suddenly. She knew what she needed to say, but didn't like the prospect of saying it aloud. Cameron regarded her keenly, waiting.

With a resigned sigh, she confessed, "I know this sounds dreadful, but I rather prefer it when we're at odds…"

Anxious about how he would respond, she was taken aback when

Cameron burst into laughter. As he laughed, she couldn't help but laugh, too. It felt good, like she'd just taken off a particularly tight pair of shoes after a long night. Or a horribly uncomfortable bra. She suddenly felt free. Relaxed. Herself.

Cameron had laughed so hard that he had to wipe away a tear. "Thank goodness!" he exclaimed. "Because I feel exactly the same way."

Perhaps, the night remained perfect in its own unpredictable way, Ellie thought.

When the cab arrived, Cameron still opened the door for her, though he had not joined her inside. He lingered in the open door, and she looked up at him. Once more, they spoke at the exact same moment. And it turns out they said the exact same word.

"Friends?"

Chapter 31: Ellie

Ellie couldn't stop thinking about Jess as she jumped into her car. Jess's voice, trembling and punctuated by sobs, echoed in her mind, repeating the words that had left Ellie feeling helpless. "It's no use, it's just hopeless. It's no use."

With every turn, Ellie's thoughts raced faster than the car could manage. What had gone wrong? She could hardly process the whirlwind of questions that buzzed in her head—what did he say? Why didn't Jess want to give it another chance? How on Earth did they leave things? Ellie remembered how she had tried to nudge Jess for more details, feeling the frustration building each time Jess had dodged her questions with heart-wrenching sobs. At that moment, she became an unwilling detective in a relationship gone awry, gathering clues from an unsolved case, desperately piecing together what this Adam bloke had done to shatter Jess's emotions.

The streetlights flickered on as dusk began to descend, cloaking the town in a romantic glow—if romance weren't currently the last thing on Ellie's mind. She imagined Adam: tall, with an unruly mop of hair and a smile that was probably irresistible when he wanted it to be. But Ellie was angry. More than anything, she was furious at him for whatever disaster had caused Jess to barrel into tears over the phone. "If only she'd just talked it through properly—maybe Jess hadn't given him a chance to defend himself!" Ellie muttered under her breath, nearly hitting a pothole as she drifted into her thoughts. "Can this day get any worse? Next, I'll find a kitten in distress!"

Just then, her phone buzzed violently in her pocket, pulling her back into reality. It was Jess again, and Ellie wouldn't let her down this time.

That she never gave Adam the chance to say something one way or the other).

Ellie has a shopping bag with several pints of ice cream in the passenger side seat. It's the only thing she knows that will help, both for her and Jess. Each had the hope of love die that night. Tonight, they were both nursing shattered hopes, love's cruel betrayal hanging heavily between them like the frigid air of winter.

She wasn't quite certain what flavours Jess preferred, so Ellie had opted for variety, filling the bag with a rainbow of choices— chunky monkey, cookies and cream, peppermint bark, and even a cheeky pint of salted caramel just because she thought it looked fancy. "Who knows," she mused whimsically, "maybe we'll have a pint-off, and I'll win with my exquisite taste in ice cream!" A silly smile broke across her face at the thought, banishing the gloom that threatened to settle like fog in her heart.

As she pulled into the supermarket car park, the memory of the checkout boy's quizzical eyebrow raised from earlier flashed in her mind. He had looked at her, weighing the absurdity of her ice cream haul against whatever notion of dietary restraint society expected. With a defiant toss of her hair, she met his gaze and declared, "You know what? I'm actually going to go grab a couple more." He might have thought her a bit mad— perhaps he had a point. But here was the secret: ice cream was Ellie's love language, a shared comfort they both needed now more than ever.

By the time she reached Jess's door, Ellie felt a surge of determination. Today was not about sadness; it was about sisterhood, laughter, and a smorgasbord of sweet solace. As she knocked, she could already envision the laughter and messy living room floor strewn with bright containers, and for a moment, just a moment, hope flickered back to life.

Heartache was hard, and she wasn't going to be shamed for handling it the only way she knew how.

Her only worry was that Chase would be hurt - it was normally his shoulder she ran to cry on. And he did love his ice cream… Ellie gripped the steering wheel tightly, her heart racing as

she parked the car along the quiet street opposite Jess's house. Her mind whirled with thoughts about the icy treat she was holding in her bag, just a few minutes away from melting into a gooey mess. She sighed dramatically as she began to gather her ice cream, crushed cones and tubs spilling over the sides, until suddenly, the radio crackled to life.

"Hold on, folks! We have a caller on the line who has something he desperately needs to say," the DJ announced with an exaggerated enthusiasm that made Ellie roll her eyes — she just wanted her ice cream!

But her bag was heavier than expected, and as she fumbled with it, the weight proved too much. A sharp tear echoed through the car as the shoulder strap ripped, sending pints of mint choc-chip and raspberry ripple flying across the floor. "Oh no!" she gasped, reaching down to salvage her treat. Amidst the chaos of flinging ice cream, the unmistakable voice wafted through the speakers.

"Jess, I don't know how to say this without sounding ridiculous, but I'm in love with you!"

Ellie's heart stopped. It was Adam! Her jaw dropped as she froze, ice cream in hand, staring at the radio in disbelief.

Ellie pops open the ice cream and eats as she listens, shocked as

Adam professes his love to Jess over the radio. He explains that this was the only way he knew how to get in touch with her since she kept avoiding him (ah ha, Ellie thinks... so there was more to the story than Jess let on).

Adam says that he didn't realise it till she said it out loud to him the other day, but he sees now that he always felt that way, too. He's just been too dumb to see it! But he sees it now.

If she would only just open the door for him...

Adam leant against the wooden fence outside Jess's house, his heart pounding like a drum in a ceilidh. "I didn't realise," he murmured to himself, recalling Jess's words just a few days ago. The way she'd looked at him, with those sparkling green eyes, had struck a chord in him. "I didn't see it until she said it out loud. It's as if the fog has lifted, and I can finally see the light!" He scratched the back of his head, feeling like a right numpty for not recognising his feelings sooner. But there it was—plain as day. "I've always felt that way," he sighed, kicking at a small stone on the path.

If only Jess would just open the door to him! He chuckled at the thought, picturing her swinging the front door wide, her smile lighting up the dim hallway like the first rays of sunshine on a Scottish spring morning. "Oh Adam, come in for a cuppa!" he imagined her saying, followed by a teasing laugh. If only it were that simple.

Meanwhile, Jess was watching from the window, her heart fluttering like a bird trapped in a cage. She mused over Adam's words, her mind racing. "He means the door to my heart," she thought, gripping the curtain as colour rushed to her cheeks. Just as she began to dream of what it might be like to finally let him in, her fantasy was abruptly interrupted.

"Ding-dong!" The doorbell rang, shattering the moment. Jess threw a nervous glance towards the front door, her heart racing once again. "Who on earth could that be?" she wondered, her stomach twisted in knots.

Then, out of nowhere, a man dashed up the steps, looking as if he had just completed the Edinburgh Marathon. "It can't be…" she breathed, her eyes widening in disbelief. "Is that Adam?"

There he stood, a whirlwind of excitement, the scent of that gorgeous aftershave he knew Jess loved hanging in the air. He pressed the doorbell again, impatiently, as though the door had magically transformed into a fortress. "Come on, open up!" he seemed to plead, a mixture of desperation and hope etched on his face.

Jess's heart danced in her chest. Perhaps today was the day. Perhaps today was the day she would finally let him in—literally and figuratively.

Ellie had a big mouthful of ice cream, and it was like watching a romantic movie as Jess opened the door. Adam hurried in, and through the living room window, Ellie watched him spin her around in his arms as they kissed.

Ellie to Chase: In the mood for ice cream. I've got a lot of it.

C to E: Again?

E to C: Yes, again.

E to C: Does that mean you don't want any? C to E: Get over here, girl.

C to E: You know I'm always in the mood for ice cream.

C to E: And you know I'm always there with a shoulder to cry on.

Ellie put the spoon in her mouth, sighing. She turned on her car and drove away, a small, happy smile on her lips.

Posted: 7:22 AM (GMT)

User: Your Fashion Ellie-vator Subscribers: 342

Three out of four ain't bad. Right!

Good morning, you! Yes, you, Gorgeous! Gor-ge-OUS, all 342 of you!

It's me, with your favourite fashion blogger who infamously swore off all love forever and ever. Well, dear ladies, I have a confession: I broke my forswearing just a teeny, tiny bit. It's hardly even worth mentioning, really. It's not like I started looking up wedding dresses online, staying up to the wee hours of the morning. I didn't put down any deposits on venues. I just… well, alright, I might have considered happily ever after for an afternoon or two.

But that's it!

Why am I even talking about myself anyway? Why hear another sob story when you could hear not one, not two, but three success stories? I've had the immense pleasure of getting to know three wonderful customers very well recently. And it's been an honour following their ups and downs on the waves of love these last few weeks since Shoperapy's grand opening.

When G came to me (or really I came to her), she was young and insecure and stuck on puppy love that did nothing but bite her and chew up her cute shoes and do its business all over her life. But I'm happy to report she's found a new pride and confidence with a man who risked sugar crashes day in and day out to prove he cared about her. It took G accepting that she was worth it, just like she was worth the silver heels that started it all. When I first met V, I saw the physique of a fitness influencer, but all she saw was the failures her ex-husband pointed out. If you see her around town, I promise you'll see her flaunting her arms in a fabulous dress. On those arms will be nothing but a sun-kissed tan and a hunky man who only ever saw her as drop-dead gorgeous.

When a friend dragged J into my shop (thank you again, C – I couldn't have done any of this without you!), she was stuck in the friend zone and could see no way out of it. But she discovered that the problem wasn't that her coworker didn't feel the same; it was her fear that he didn't. I can't say for sure a new dress solved everything, but it certainly didn't hurt as it was exactly what she was wearing when he twirled her around after practically knocking down her door to finally kiss her.

So there you have it, dear readers. Love, love, and more love. (Not for me, of course, because I'm done with all that.)

It's time to help more women find their way to their one and only (or their one and only for the night…). Don't let my lucklessness deter you. Think of it like I'm saving all my luck for you and your precious heart.

Whether you need a new pair of shoes or a pair of ears to listen to your woes, I'm here for you. And the community we're building at Shoperapy is here for you, too.

So… who's next, darlings?

See you all very soon, my gorgeous, fashionable friends!

Love Ellie x

Chapter 32: Victoria

Victoria had finally managed to drag Ellie to the gym. To say that Ellie was reluctant would be a grave understatement; it was as if someone had suggested taking her prized fuchsia velvet gown for a jog. "Look, Vic," she whined, running a manicured hand through her perfectly styled hair, "hanging up all of my designer gowns is already a workout. You should see me on a Saturday night; I practically lift weights - those sequins are heavy!"

Victoria stifled a giggle as she looked at her friend. "But how much do those 'exercises' actually make you sweat?" she teased, her running shoes squeaking slightly against the gym's polished floor.

"Sweat?" Ellie exclaimed with wide eyes, as if the word itself was a slap in the face. "Darling, I never sweat in Gucci. If I should somehow start glistening, I might have to consider a career change as a hot mess!"

With a determined look, Victoria marched towards the weight section. "Well, It was either lift these weights or stand there looking fabulous while holding up the wall! Your call."

Ellie sniffed, eyeing the dumbbells as though they were venomous snakes. "Physical exertion is simply not in my DNA. Besides, these weights wouldn't complement my evening wear. Should I coordinate with them first? It was rather tragic when everything clashed!"

"Ellie," Victoria said, suppressing a laugh, "the only thing tragic here is your refusal to break a sweat. A little perspiration can do wonders for your skin!"

Ellie exclaimed dramatically, "Perspiration? How daring! Next, you'll be suggesting I wear joggers with my prized boutique collection!"

Victoria chuckled as she took a lightweight, demonstrating excellent form despite her friend's protests. "You might actually enjoy it! Plus, think of it as an extension of your fashion sense: each lunge could be a new pose!"

"Fine," Ellie finally relented, rolling her eyes but unable to hide a smile. "But if I start to sweat, I'm blaming you. And I might just have to bring the gym my entire wardrobe for a fashion show!"

Victoria asked how much those 'exercises' made Ellie sweat. "Sweat?" Ellie exclaimed. "I never sweat in Gucci."

In the end, Victoria agreed to model some clothes for pictures for the Shoperapy website so that Ellie could finally go to the gym with her.

She expected to hear some grumbling from Ellie, but it is nothing compared to all the complaining Ellie is actually doing. "Right, that was a pretty good workout," Ellie declared, panting slightly as she leaned against the wall, wiping the sweat from her brow with the back of her hand. "So, what are we having for lunch? Shrimp tacos? Because I could absolutely demolish some right now!"

Victoria chuckled, her brow barely glistening as she adjusted her ponytail. "Hold on, Ellie! You've got to stop on your way to the locker room." With a gentle nudge, she prevented Ellie from zipping off to celebrate what was just the beginning of their exercise.

"Wait, that was only half the warmup?" Ellie blinked in

astonishment, her mouth agape like a fish out of water. "Half? You've got to be kidding me!"

"Yep," Victoria replied teasingly, suppressing a laugh. "We haven't even hit the real workout! Just think of it as a gentle tickle before the full onslaught."

Ellie's eyes widened comically, betraying a mix of horror and disbelief. "Gentle tickle? This feels like a full-on circus performance where I'm the clown trying to juggle while running a marathon!" She flailed her arms a bit, half-laughing and half-exasperated.

"Just a couple more minutes of this 'gentle tickle,' and then we can get into the fun stuff!" Victoria turned on some upbeat music, practically bouncing in place, brimming with energy.

"Fun stuff? I thought we were doing cardio, not signing up for a dance-off on the telly!" Ellie exclaimed, her voice rising, hinting at playful outrage.

Victoria grinned, effortlessly jumping into a series of burpees while Ellie struggled to keep up, her feet moving more like a giraffe on roller skates.

"See, this is how you unleash the magic of the workout!" Victoria encouraged, hardly breaking a sweat. "Come on, Ellie! Think of those shrimp tacos! Each burpee brings us closer!"

With a dramatic sigh, Ellie tried to push herself through the next round. "If I don't get those tacos soon, I might just faint from sheer exhaustion – or worse, faint and dream about them!" Victoria doubled over in laughter, clearly enjoying the antics of her best friend. "Well then, let's hurry and finish this warmup!

Tacos await you!"

Victoria led Ellie to the Ski Machine and watched as Ellie struggled the whole time while Ellie noticed Victoria was hardly even breathing hard.

"Victoria," Ellie leaned over on the treadmill to whisper, "I'm starting to sweat."

"Good!" Victoria said, pushing up the speed on the treadmill. It made Ellie go into the tiniest jog.

"Are you crazy??" Victoria laughs.

Ellie really should not have had so much ice cream the night before with Chase. And crying really is very dehydrating, isn't it? Could she get a doctor's note to get out of working out with her Victoria?

Soon, Victoria runs on her treadmill while Ellie's 'catching her breath', aka not moving at all.

Victoria started to update Ellie on her new romance. "You won't believe what's happened with Levi!" she exclaimed, her voice bubbling with enthusiasm. "I mean, I've hardly believed it myself!" A few coy strands of hair fell across her brow as she tried to push them back, her cheeks tinged a rosy hue.

Ellie raised an eyebrow, curiosity piqued. "Oh? Do tell!" She leaned in, intrigued by the excitement that shrouded Victoria's words.

"Well, we went swimming at the beach last weekend. And let me tell you, the water was freezing, but… it was all sorts of fun! I could hardly focus on the cold when Levi kept stealing glances—like he was somehow captivated. Can you imagine?" Victoria twirled a piece of grass nervously. "Then there was the sauna mishap."

"Oh no, what did you do?" Ellie stifled a laugh, as if preparing for a story worthy of a soap opera.

Victoria's expression was a blend of laughter and exasperation. "So, there we were, post-swim, feeling warm and slightly smug about our daring beach escapade. And in that sauna, being all glowy and lovely, I thought, 'Who needs to wear a full ensemble?'" She rolled her eyes, the memory making her chuckle. "Then, just as I was settling in, I slipped, and suddenly I was only in my sports bra like some sort of bathing suit model from the May issue of Vogue!"

"And what did he do?" Ellie barely managed to suppress her laughter.

"He simply laughed! It is not the kind of mocking laughter, but more like the kind that says, 'Wow, you're brave!' It suddenly struck me that I didn't need the 'perfect' body to be liked. I mean, I was so fixated on being a flawless version of myself that I was the one shutting doors before they even had a chance to open. So, let's just say, I'm five steps ahead with Levi now, and It was creeping me out in the best way possible!"

"I had it in my mind that I had to have this perfect body before a man ever liked me again. And I was closing myself off to people and opportunities, because I didn't feel like I was 'there' yet."

Victoria explained that it was no big deal that Levi saw her body so quickly - it made no difference to him (not that he didn't find her gorgeous), because he already knew he liked her and wanted to be with her when she gave her big speech about what she was looking for in love at her age.

It all worked out exactly as it should have in the end.

"And that reminds me," Victoria says, "I want to try on that new strapless dress you got in, for an upcoming date with Levi." The clatter of free weights echoed through the gym like a mechanical symphony, punctuated by Ellie's breathless whines. "Is it time for margaritas yet?" she panted, her grip on the dumbbells dangerously loose. With every repetition, she winced as if the weights were made of solid lead rather than the sleek plastic-coated versions they truly were.

Meanwhile, Cameron walked over, his gym-junkie confidence radiating off him like a beacon. He observed Ellie's form with an eyebrow raised, like a gym critic inspecting a culinary disaster. "Ellie, love," he began, suppressing a chuckle, "that's not quite how It was done. You might want to straighten your back a bit."

Ellie's eyes widened, incredulous. "Are you kidding me? This is perfect. My back feels just dandy!" She thrust the weights upward, a look of fierce determination crossing her face. Her voice was a crescendo of defiance, drowned only by the clanking of metal on metal.

Victoria, positioned nearby, stifled a laugh behind a carefully crafted façade of composure. She'd seen her best friend's form; it was the gym equivalent of trying to bake a soufflé inside a tyre. But today, she decided silence was golden, perhaps even more so than Ellie's current form. A small grin tugged at her lips, barely contained as she watched the scene unfold.

Cameron smirked, his arms crossed. "I'll give you an A for effort, but your back could use a little—oh, what's the term? Ah yes, support'." He gestured dramatically, adding a delayed clap for effect.

"Oh please, Cameron, I'm not made of glass!" Ellie protested, her expression switching from indignation to amusement. The two were a perfect comedy duo—the critique, the counterpoint. As they shared a laugh, even Victoria couldn't resist joining in, her grin stretching wider.

She listened to Ellie and Cameron's banter, which they both seemed to enjoy.

Cameron gave Ellie a wink when he left.

"Things are going well between you then?" Victoria asks. "Oh, they're going horribly," Ellie says, laughing. "Just the way we like it."

It would never work out between them, but it was better that way. Besides, Ellie had sworn off love – didn't Victoria remember? And she had Shoperapy and the women who came in for help - her true loves.

Victoria nodded, knowing it wouldn't be long till Ellie was on another break from swearing off love.

Chapter 33: Jess

Jess slowly woke up; the remnants of sleep clung to her like a long-forgotten coat. For a moment, she was wrapped in the fog of confusion, unsure of her surroundings even though she knew she was at home. The warm sunlight spilled through the blinds, tickling her bare toes, as if the sun itself envied the freedom of her feet. With a groggy blink, she attempted to piece together the puzzle of her morning.

Then it hit her like a well-timed joke – she was not cocooned in her bed but sprawled on the couch in her living room. "Right, sofa, my dear trusty companion," she chuckled to herself, recalling how last night devolved into laughter and tiredness after a marathon of conversation and wine.

But she wasn't alone. Adam's legs were sprawled beside hers, utterly relaxed, an island of calm in the sea of her chaotic thoughts. His head rested on the opposite couch cushion from hers, tousled hair creating its own form of chaos. Jess can't help but smile as she quietly watches him, wondering what dreams could possibly be brewing in that head of his, probably something ridiculous involving superpowers and sandwiches.

She felt a surge of happiness so profound it almost seemed surreal. It was the sort of happiness that seemed to bubble up from within, spilling over until she couldn't contain the grin plastered across her face. If someone were to walk in right now, they'd think she had just won a million pounds or discovered a secret portal to another world. But no, all it took is this moment, the two of them encircled in the soft morning light, to make her spirit soar like a soaring kite catching the wind.

"Just you wait, Adam," she whispered playfully, "when you wake up, I'll have to remind you how you drool like a baby hippo." It was a light-hearted tease, but a reminder of the warmth they share, built on laughter and fond memories. Today, she knew it would be one of their best, simply because of their shared night.

She was happier than she could ever remember being - she just couldn't stop smiling.

The events of the night came back to her: her radio playing as she reached for another tissue, waiting for Ellie to come over with what she promised was 'way too much ice cream', her hearing Adam's voice and being so confused and then so overwhelmed and then so joyous as she heard what he was saying to her through the radio, his knock at the door, her opening and immediately having his lips crash against hers, her feet lifting from the floor and him spinning her around and around, not even bothering to close the front door as he held her tighter and tighter.

It had been magical, all of it. A dream that she found was still there when she woke up.

Jess and Adam had spent the entire night talking, their every word unravelling the tightly woven fabric of unspoken feelings. Sitting in Jess's tiny flat, she leaned precariously on the battered sofa while Adam sprawled on the floor, the remnants of their laughter echoing in the dim light. A bottle of wine clinked against another, remnants of their cheeky decision to indulge a little too much.

"Remember when you tried to dance at that wedding?" Jess giggled, tossing her hair back, an exaggerated gesture. "I thought you were attempting to communicate with aliens!" Adam chortled, pretending to adjust an invisible antenna, his face contorted into an assortment of goofy expressions. Their laughter was rich and infectious, each chuckle filled with the electricity of their shared history, now tinged with the possibility of something more.

The wine had worked its magic, slowly softening the barriers they had so carefully maintained. With every sip, their revelations spilt out even quicker than the last few drops from the bottle. "Do you think we've been blind, you know, to each other?" Adam asked, his tone suddenly serious, though a sly smirk played at the corners of his mouth, attempting to cloak his vulnerability. Jess nodded, a playful glint in her eye.

"Yes! You were like a deer in headlights! I was right here, waving my arms!" she teased, imitating a frantic dance of desperation.

Adam laughed again, his shoulders shaking, already half-drowning in the affection that had blossomed over years of friendship. They ended their night by boldly discussing dreams — big, audacious dreams. The prospect of moving in together danced through the air like fairy lights, illuminating their future with soft promises.

"Marriage, babies... the whole shebang!" he grinned, his eyes widening theatrically. Jess gasped, feigning shock, "Next, you'll suggest we get a cat!"

As they exchanged conspiratorial smirks, the night felt electric with potential. It was clear that this was just the beginning of a beautifully messy adventure.

Jess couldn't believe how quickly they made plans for the future - neither were afraid to talk about big, serious relationship things like moving, marriage, even babies.

It was like everything had just fallen into perfect place after all those years of being 'just friends'. The night could not have gone better.

Jess didn't want to wake Adam up - they were up very late, and he looked so cute sleeping so contentedly.

Jess slipped free from her blanket and slowly tiptoed into the kitchen, careful not to make a sound. The sun gently filtered through the window, casting a warm glow on the wooden surfaces. Today was a special day; she wanted to surprise Adam with a delightful breakfast. As she stood at the counter, her excitement bubbled up inside her.

With a sharp knife in hand, Jess started slicing fresh fruit— ripe bananas, juicy strawberries, and tangy apples. The vibrant colours of the fruit made the kitchen feel lively and inviting. Next, she gathered the ingredients for pancake batter: flour, eggs, milk, and a sprinkle of baking powder. Methodically, she measured each ingredient, ensuring that today's pancakes would be fluffy and light.

A warm smile spread across her face at the thought of Adam enjoying her homemade breakfast. She enjoyed those quiet moments in the kitchen, where each sound, the whisper of the knife, the clatter of bowls—brought her a sense of peace.

"Just a little longer," she thought as she lifted a juicer above a bowl, squeezing the bright oranges to make fresh juice. The sweet and zesty smell filled the air, bringing a sense of freshness that was hard to resist.

Once everything was prepped, Jess looked at the clock; Adam would be waking soon. She decided to wait before turning on the griddle, wanting him to savour warm pancakes when he finally stirred. She took a deep breath and savoured the anticipation, ready to create a lovely start to their day together.

So, she made herself a cup of coffee and sat cross-legged with her laptop at her kitchen table. She knew that there was someone she needed to thank for all that had happened. And she wanted to give the biggest, best thanks she could.

Jess pulled up the Internet, navigated to the right page, and, with a smile on her face, began to write and write...

Everyone needs to visit Shoperapy

As I stepped into Ellie's boutique, I felt a sense of warmth surrounding me, as though I had been welcomed into a friend's home rather than a fashion boutique. From the moment I walked through the door, I was struck by the beautiful layout of the store, adorned with stunning displays that showcased a carefully curated selection of clothing and accessories. Each garment seemed to tell its own unique story, and I could hardly contain my excitement as I browsed through the vibrant racks. Ellie had truly created a space that felt alive with possibilities.

Ellie herself stands out not only for her impeccable sense of style but also for her genuine passion for fashion and the empowerment of women. When I approached her for assistance, I was immediately struck by her sincerity. Rather than pushing sales on me, she took the time to understand my personal style and offered thoughtful suggestions that complemented my figure and colour preferences. This level of attentiveness is a rarity in many shopping experiences and made me feel valued as a customer. Ellie's expertise shines through as she shares her incredible insights on what works best for various body types, encouraging us all to embrace our individual shapes.

What truly sets Ellie's boutique apart is the community of women she had fostered within those four walls. Walking through the shop, I noticed how women of all ages were mingling, sharing their thoughts about different outfits, and offering one another compliments. It felt like a supportive sisterhood, where every woman felt free to express her thoughts without judgement. This nurturing environment is a testament to Ellie's vision; she believes that fashion is not just about clothing but about building confidence and friendships.

One of the most touching aspects of my experience was witnessing how Ellie embraces every woman who comes into her shop with open arms. She had created not only a shopping destination but also a haven where women could seek advice on their wardrobes and feel uplifted. It was heart-warming to see how Ellie took the time to chat with her customers, encouraging them to step outside their comfort zones while celebrating their unique styles. She believes that fashion should bring joy, and her boutique is a reflection of that philosophy. After spending a delightful afternoon in her shop, I decided to try on several pieces, each of which offered a fresh perspective on my wardrobe options. I felt liberated as I twirled in front of the mirror, admiring how the dresses accented my curves and allowed me to express my personality. Ellie was right there by my side, cheering me on and encouraging me to try on styles that I would typically shy away from. It was refreshing to have someone who genuinely wants to uplift women, not only through fashion but also through self-acceptance.

I wholeheartedly recommend Ellie's Boutique to all women who are seeking not only assistance with their wardrobe but a little encouragement for their hearts as well. The spirit of camaraderie among the women who visit is incredible, and the transformative experience Ellie offers is something that should not be missed. Whether you feel stuck in a fashion rut, are looking for the perfect outfit for a special occasion, or simply want to surround yourself with supportive women, Ellie's shop is the place to be. The harmonious blend of community, fashion, and empowerment truly earns this boutique a solid five-star review. Visit Shoperapy—you won't just leave with a bag of clothes, but a skip in your step and perhaps a new friend or two along the way or like me… you might even find love.

Jess x

Chapter 34: Ellie

Ellie was closing the shop a few days later. It had been her busiest day so far. She reminded herself that she needed to send Jess a thankyou card - she knew how valuable her raving review was to the store's success today. It was still a long uphill road to building a long-term business. Ellie knew this now: there was no easy way to succeed — but she could see the progress she'd made, and she was determined – she was in it for the long haul. No giving up! Despite the challenges, she felt her efforts were beginning to pay off, and that the shop might indeed prove a great success.

Ellie clapped her hands, and her heart raced with excitement. "This is it!" she exclaimed, her eyes sparkling as she gazed around her very own boutique. With these stunning clothes and accessories, I'm not only going to build a successful business for myself but also help women find the perfect outfit for the perfect date along the way. I can just see it—a shop filled with laughter, with women falling in love, not only with the clothes but with the entire experience and even maybe falling in love with… the one. A girl can dream, Ellie laughed to herself.

Just as Ellie shifted the sign on the front door from 'Open' to 'Closed', the sudden sound of a knock reverberated through the hushed atmosphere of her quaint little shop. Outside, a figure stood under the flickering shop light.

Memories flashed vividly through her mind—a reminder of that fateful night when Cameron had burst through the door with infectious enthusiasm and reckless charm, commanding the entire room with his vibrant energy. At that moment, beneath the sparkly lights that adorned her shop, she had thought he might be 'the one' to break through her guarded heart. But, as those naive dreams crumbled into dust, the notion of romantic destiny had become a bittersweet memory, one she had long since shoved deep within her psyche. She felt almost immune to the idea now, a conviction settling in her soul that no such person was destined to cross her path.

Eliie opened the door. The man's youthful look was glaringly apparent, marked by the dirt that clung stubbornly to his skin—unshaven, burnt by the relentless sun, and giving out an unpleasant smell that suggested he had wandered far too long without care. His eyes, however, glinted with a flicker of desperation, possibly a reminder of something lost.

"What do you want?" she muttered, her tone brusque and unwelcoming, jagged as the broken pavement outside her boutique.

"Um, yeah, I'm looking for my chick. I was told she shops here or something... But I might be wrong, 'cos she's got no money, and this looks like pricey chick stuff." His words spilled out, awkward and clumsy.

With her arms crossed defiantly, Ellie stood her ground, the shadows coiling protectively around her like an audience poised in bated breath, filled with suspense, waiting to witness the outcome of this uninvited encounter.

Without hesitation, Ellie immediately put it all together, and immediately knew who this disagreeable man was. And she immediately didn't like him.

"Let me take a guess," she remarked, a hint of sarcasm lacing her tone, "You must be Tim?"

Tim, taken aback by her immediate recognition, replied with an expression of surprise, "That's correct. But I must ask, is she here or what?"

Ellie raised an eyebrow, sensing his lack of familiarity. "Are you referring to Grace?" she inquired with a more inquisitive tone.

"Yes, exactly, her!" he responded eagerly. "I'm here to surprise her!"

"How lovely for you," Ellie replied, her voice dripping with sarcasm as she felt irritation rising within her like steam in a kettle.

"Look, can you just tell me if she's here? I don't want to miss her," Tim insisted, his desperation palpable and almost as thick as the air in the shop.

Ellie hesitated, weighing her words carefully. Grace had always been one to chase after fleeting moments like moths to a flame, but Tim? He didn't strike her as worthy of Grace's affection, more like a stain on her friend's life than a soulmate. "Why don't you find a nice bar and wait for her there?" Ellie suggested, her tone still edged with prickliness.

Tim blinked, clearly confused. "What do you mean? She must be here somewhere! Look, if she's with someone, that would be... well, that would suck, but..." "Look," Ellie interrupted, finally losing her patience. "Grace doesn't need this kind of surprise. You used to mean something to her, but those days are gone. Maybe it is best if you let her be."

"What do you know?" Tim countered, his voice rising. "I'm here to make things right. To show her I care!"

Her eyes narrowed. "By showing up unannounced like a bad penny after you ran off to Thailand to find yourself. What do you think that'll achieve? Do you want to surprise her? Surprise her then by letting her have a life without you barging back in. Grace has never been happier in the last few months, you know." The tension between them was thick. Tim shifted uncomfortably, clearly at a loss for words.

"Yeah, well, I just…" he began, but uncertainty stammered through his lips.

Ellie sighed, her voice softening. "Look, Tim, you've got to understand something. Grace deserves to be treated with respect. If you really care, give her space. Let her be who she is without your shadow looming over her."

Their eyes locked in a moment that felt electric — Tim being hit with a realisation of truth. For a fleeting second, something like understanding flickered in Tim's eyes, but just as quickly, it was extinguished by his defiance.

"She needs to know I'm here. She should know how I feel!" he retorted, stubbornness creeping back into his tone.

"And she will," Ellie replied firmly. "But not like this. You need to show patience, not desperation."

Realisation settled heavily within the hush. A tenuous possibility hung in the air, teetering on the edge for both of them.

"In time," she added gently, "if it was meant to be, she will find her way back to you." But not if she had any sense, she thought to herself. "Now, you'd best get going", Ellie said, softening her posture.

With a final hesitant glance, Tim turned and stepped out into the cool night air, the shadows closing in behind him.

Before he could say anything else, Ellie closed the door in his face.

And locked it.

Ellie had never wanted to strangle a man more. She knew that a few weeks ago, Grace would have died for this very exact moment to come true. Tim was her whole life. She couldn't see past him, even if he had nothing to see past at all. She was totally stuck on a guy who was rude and unkind.

But thanks to Ellie and her charming boutique, Grace had found herself in the company of a gentleman—a man who truly valued her. Someone who offered her respect and companionship. Unlike Tim, he wouldn't simply escape to Thailand and return whenever it pleased him.

Ellie stood alone in her shop, letting out a wistful sigh. Perhaps tomorrow would bring better surprises.

This was precisely why she had opened her fashion boutique: to empower women, to stand beside them, and to illuminate their paths as they navigated the often-rocky quest for true love. Yet, standing in the shadows of her own vulnerability, she was resolutely certain that there was no way she would have divulged to Tim how to find Grace.

Just then, Chase appeared from the back room, where he had been helping Ellie tidy away remnants of her busy shop. He shook his head, disbelief etched across his face. "Who was that?" he asked, leaning against the counter and crossing his arms, curiosity creeping into his voice.

Ellie turned to him, a playful smirk on her lips that couldn't be contained. "No one," she replied, with a mischievous twinkle in her eye.

She spun around, her rainbow pleated skirt swirling around her like a whirlwind of colour, as she moved towards the full-length mirror, admiring her latest fashion.

"What a busy day?" she continued, enthusiasm pouring out of her as she waved her arm dramatically. "Lots of happy customers with beautiful outfits from my boutique." She continued, "Hopefully, they will all come back for more soon and, with their friends in toe."

Chase chuckled, his scepticism fading as he watched her. "You do realise that while the clothes might catch their attention, it is your personality that will keep them coming back, right?" He leaned back with an amused grin, clearly enjoying Ellie's happiness.

"Of course!" Ellie laughed, her enthusiasm unwavering. "But why not let my fashion do the talking first? It was the

best introduction I could offer! Besides, who wouldn't want to wear something that reflects their imagination?"

She turned again to face Chase, her hands animated as she spoke. "I envision a world where everyone feels confident and beautiful in clothes and accessories from Shoperapy!"

"Exactly," Chase said smiling, nodding as he studied her twirl, the reflection of her dreams bright in her eyes.

"But just remember what you said; it was not all about the clothes. It was your connection with them, too; you established a personal bond with all your customers that made them feel special." His tone suddenly turned serious, imparting the wisdom of experience.

Ellie affirmed, her gaze shifting from the mirror back to Chase, appreciating his support amidst all the glamour and hustle. "I know the importance of relationships in business. It is about creating a community, where people feel like they belong. That's my ultimate goal."

As they both shared a knowing look, Ellie's heart swelled with gratitude for her friend who understood her vision. "I'm going to continue to make this shop a place where fashion meets friendship," she declared, determination glinting in her eyes. The air vibrated with her dreams, promising a future painted in vibrant colours.

"Now then," she said, "It was time to celebrate; where's that champagne?"

Chase grinned and pulled a bottle and two champagne flutes from behind his back.

"Way ahead of you, sister."

Printed in Dunstable, United Kingdom